A Brief Guide

ISLAM

BELIEF AND PRACTICE

A Brief Guide

ISLAM

BELIEF AND PRACTICE

Süleyman Eriş

The Light

New Jersey
2006

Published by The Light, Inc.
26 Worlds Fair Dr. Suite C
Somerset, New Jersey, 08873, USA

www.thelightpublishing.com

Library of Congress Cataloging-in-Publication Data

Eris, Suleyman.
  Islam : belief and practice : a brief guide / Suleyman Eris. -- 1st ed.
    p. cm.
  ISBN 1-59784-051-3
  1. Islam--Doctrines. 2. Islam--Islam--Customs and practices.
I. Title.
BP165.5.E75 2006
297--dc22

                                                       2006012997

Printed by
Çaglayan A.S., Izmir - Turkey
June 2006

TABLE OF CONTENTS

Preface vii

ISLAM - THE UNIVERSAL FAITH

The Purpose of Life and Belief...3
    The divine purposes for creating humanity and the world.............5
    A parable on the divine purposes of creation...................................6
Islamic View of Mankind 13
    God's vicegerent on earth...13
    All human beings are equal..15
The Prophet Muhammad..17
    The Prophet's homeland 17
    Muhammad's life before his prophethood.........................19
    Mission...21
    Muhammad as a Messenger of God....................................21
    Commitment to the call...23
    What was his message? 27
The Qur'an...31
    Earlier Divine Revelations and the Qur'an.......................31
    Defining the Qur'an 32
    Arguments for the Qur'an's divine authorship...............34
    Recording and preserving the Qur'an 36
Islamic Civilization 39

BELIEF - SIX PILLARS

One True God..46
Angels 48
Books - Divine Scriptures 51

Prophets 53
The Resurrection and the Afterlife 57
Divine Decree and Destiny 58

PRACTICE - FIVE PILLARS

Declaration of Faith 63
Prayer - Daily Worship 65
    Bath (*Ghusl*) - Major ablution 68
    Wudu - Minor ablution 69
    Tayammum - Ablution with clean soil 70
    Requirements of a prayer 70
    Conditions of prayer 70
    Obligatory acts or the pillars of prayer 71
    The performance of prayer - a two-cycle example 71
Fast of Ramadan 74
Purifying Alms (*zakat*) 77
Pilgrimage - The Hajj 78
    A short description of the rites 80

Conclusion 82
Addendum I - Forbidden and Lawful 83
Addendum II - Islam and Culture 85
Addendum III - How to Perform Prescribed Prayers 87

About the author 91
Notes 95

PREFACE

All praise is for God and may God's blessings and peace be upon His Messenger Muhammad. This book is intended to open a small window into Islamic belief and practice in order to assist beginners desiring to learn the basics of Islam.

The book consists of three chapters. Islam – The Universal Faith presents an overview of the Islamic worldview. It addresses stimulating questions such as, "Who am I?" and "What am I doing in this world?" It delivers solid information from Islamic tradition in order to answer those questions. Additionally, a small biography of the Prophet Muhammad is given to help the reader acquire an historical perspective of his role in Islam. Next The Qur'an and some of its aspects regarding its divine authorship and preservation are introduced. Finally, Islamic Civilization is discussed with a retrospect into history, and is accompanied by commentaries of Western scholars.

The second chapter delves into Islamic belief and its six pillars: belief in God, the prophets, the divinely revealed books, angels, resurrection, and divine destiny. The rationality of Islamic belief is explained with reference to verses from The Qur'an and prophetic sayings. Parables and commentaries by Bediüzzaman Said Nursi enrich the content and help facilitate comprehension.

The third chapter discusses practices of the Islamic faith, which are defined as "the five pillars of Islam." While the previous chapter focused on the conviction of the heart, this section, in a sense, provides information regarding the outward form of the religion: declaration of faith, prescribed daily prayers, fasting, purifying alms, pilgrimage. Texts of some of verses and prayers are available at the end of the book, with photographs demonstrating how to perform the daily ritual prayers.

I would like to thank the following friends who contributed to this book with their useful advice, editing, and comments: Ali Ünal, Bonnie Rutherford Shahin, Kathleen St. Onge, Jane Louise Kandur, Ahmet Kurucan, and Hüseyin Şentürk.

Islam – The Universal Faith

- ➤ The Purpose of Life and Belief
- ➤ Islamic View of Mankind
- ➤ The Prophet Muhammad
- ➤ The Qur'an
- ➤ Islamic Civilization

THE PURPOSE OF LIFE AND BELIEF

Who am I? Where do I come from? What is my final destination? What does death demand from me? Who is my guide on this journey?

It is in all of these questions that the essential problem of human life lies, and our individual and collective happiness requires being able to give the correct answer to the vital questions mentioned, as well as in disciplining our faculties so that we may produce a harmonious, peaceful individual and social life. Since it is not possible for the human intellect to totally comprehend where true human happiness lies, in both this world and the next, humanity needs a universal intellect, a guidance from beyond human reason and experience, to whose authority all may assent freely. That guidance is the religion revealed and perfected by God through His Prophets.[1] With Islam, God completed the religion He revealed and chose for humanity:

> This day I have perfected your religion for you, completed My Favor upon you, and have chosen for you Islam as your religion. (Maidah 5:3)

Islam means "submission to God, peace, and salvation." It is only through submission to God that one can attain the peace in both individual and social spheres, and salvation in both this world and the next. This is why all the prophets came with the same doctrine of faith, the same precepts of worship and good conduct, and the same principles for regulating social life. It is only in some secondary matters of law that they differed; and this was only in connection with the time and conditions in which they lived.

The name of the religion that encompasses this doctrine and these precepts and principles is Islam. Names of other religions were given by either their followers or by their opponents, and they were given some time after their messengers had left this world. Islam is the eternal religion and it brings nothing that is fundamentally new; instead it has come to re-establish the primordial religion, and to reaffirm the Truth, which is beyond time. As a re-establishment and a reaffirmation, Islam is a synthesis of the universal Revelation: it is the recapitulation of all the previous messages which Heaven has vouch-safed mankind. It is this which gives it its astonishing capacity to integrate, within a single community, believers of very different ethnic origins, while still respecting their particularities.[2]

All the prophets came with Islam and communicated this message, but their followers failed to observe and preserve it, making changes to it over time. It was communicated for the final time by the Prophet Muhammad, peace and blessings be upon him, in a way that would embrace all people until the end of time. So it is only "the Islam" which the Prophet Muhammad preached that is approved by God as the true religion:

> Say (O Messenger): "We have believed in God (without associating any partners with Him), and that which has been sent down on us, and that which was sent down on Abraham, Ishmael, Isaac, Jacob and the Prophets who were raised in the tribes, and that which was given to Moses, Jesus, and all other Prophets from their Lord; we make no distinction between any of them (in believing), and we are Muslims (submitted to Him wholly and exclusively). (Al Imran 3:84)

It is important to note that the Prophet Muhammad is not the founder of Islam, but the Messenger of Islam. Islam is the natural way of life. God is the originator of Islam, and Adam, the first person on earth, is the first Muslim. Likewise, the Prophet Abraham, who lived 2,500 years before the Prophet Muhammad, is called a Muslim in the Qur'an (Al Imran 3:60). All the prophets carried the same message from God—the message of Islam, of peace and piety.[3]

In its most fundamental aspect, Islam is epitomized in the most frequently recited of all Qur'anic phrases, the Basmala or Bismillahir-rahmanir-rahim—"In the name of God, The Merciful, The Compassionate." God manifests Himself via His absolute, all-inclusive Mercy and Compassion, and Islam is founded upon that affirmation. The Qur'an calls the Prophet Muhammad's mission *a mercy for all the worlds* (Hajj 21:107).[4]

THE DIVINE PURPOSES FOR CREATING HUMANITY AND THE WORLD

Since the One God is Infinite and Absolute as well as the Infinitely Good, He could not but create. His infinitude implies that He contains within Himself all possibilities, and such possibility had to be realized in the form of creation. It is in the nature of the good to give of itself, and the Infinitely-Good could not but radiate the reality that constitutes the world.[5]

> We have not created the heavens and the earth and all that is between them in vain (so that people should think themselves at liberty to act each according to his own desires and inclinations). (Sad 38:27)

The following sacred saying, *hadith qudsi*,[6] explains the deepest purpose of creation which is God's love for the knowledge of Himself being realized through His vicegerent on earth: humanity.

> "I was a hidden treasure. I loved to be known. Therefore, I created the creation so that I would be known."

For a human being to know God is to fulfill the purpose of creation. In order to understand the divine purposes for creating humanity and the universe, the following parable from Bediüzzaman Said Nursi is helpful.[7] Bediüzzaman (1877-1960) is one of the leading scholars of Islam whose *Risale-i Nur* (Treatise of Light) Collection has been extensively studied among Muslims, especially in Turkey. Risale-i Nur is regarded as a modern interpretation of the Qur'an which provides most convincing arguments for the Islamic articles of faith:

A PARABLE ON THE DIVINE PURPOSES OF CREATION

A king had a vast treasury of precious stones and buried treasuries known only to him. He was well versed in all industries, and had a vast knowledge of all artistic and scientific disciplines. As anyone who has beauty and perfection naturally tends to display these qualities to others[8], he wanted to build a palace that would demonstrate his kingdom's magnificence, the extent of his wealth and its splendor, and the wonderful products of his artistry and skill. He also desired to behold his beauty and perfection with his own discerning eye and through the eyes of others.

And so he began to build a very large, magnificent palace. Dividing it into many apartments and rooms, he decorated it with his finest and most beautiful works of art, and embellished it with his precious stones. Designing it according to artistic and scientific principles and disciplines, he furnished it with the miraculous products of his knowledge. Finally, he prepared delicious food and drink for each family that would live therein, and provided them so elaborately, generously, and artistically that each food seemed to be derived from at least 100 separate skills.

Then, the king settled some of his subjects in the palace. He sent his aide de camp to explain why he had built it, the rules they had to obey, what kind of being the king was, and about the palace's architecture, decorations, furniture, and ornaments. The king told his aide de camp to explain how the palace's structures, designs, and contents demonstrated his artistry and perfections, and how those dwelling in it could please him.

The aide de camp had many students, and each of his numerous assistants was deputed for a certain apartment. Standing among his students, he addressed the audience:

> O people! Our master, who owns this palace, built it to make himself known to you. In return, know and recognize him properly. He wants to make himself lovable to you through these ornaments. In return, appreciate his artistry and commend him for his works, thereby making yourselves loved by him. His favors demonstrate his love for you, so love him by obeying him. His offerings display his care and compassion for you, so thank him by showing your respect for him. Through the works of his perfection, the master wants to show his beauty and grace. In return, exhibit a great desire to see him and secure his attention. By setting his special stamp, which cannot be copied, on everything you see, he demonstrates that he is unique, absolutely independent and without partner, that this palace and its contents are his work and belong to him exclusively. So, acknowledge his uniqueness, absolute independence, and lack of partner.

The aide-de-camp continued his address. The palace's inhabitants were of two types. The people in the first group, sensible and aware of themselves, saw the palace's wonders and concluded that everything had a purpose. While thinking about this, they listened to the aide-de-camp and learned what those purposes were. They did what the king wanted, and so pleased him. In return, the king invited them to a far larger and indescribably more beautiful palace, wherein he gave them all kinds of eternal bounties and blessings.

The people in the second group were morally corrupt, unaware, and devoid of sound reasoning, for all they saw was delicious food. Also, they did not understand the meaning behind the decorations and embellishments. Ignoring the address and directives of the aide-de-camp and his assistants, they concentrated on eating and sleeping. After drinking forbidden beverages, they became drunk, bothered the servants and guests, and broke the rules. So, the king put them in prison.

In short, the glorious king built the palace for the purposes explained by his aide-de-camp. Realizing these purposes depends on two things. First, if the aide-de-camp did not exist, those purposes would be as nothing, for a book without a teacher to explain it is only a bundle of paper. Second, the aid-de-camp must be obeyed, for his existence is the reason for creating the palace, and its inhabitants' obedience is the reason for maintaining it. Without an aide-de-camp to make the palace known to its inhabitants and tell them of the king's will, the latter would not have built it. Also, if they ignore the king's instructions, the palace will be destroyed.

If you understand this, reflect upon its meaning. The palace is this world, whose roof is the heavens illuminated with smiling stars, whose floor is earth's surface embellished with numerous kinds of flowers. The king is God, the Most Holy One, the Eternal King, Whom the seven firmaments and earth, along with all their contents, glorify and extol in tongues particular to each. He is such a Powerful King that He created the heavens and earth in 6 days.[9] Seated on His Throne of Lordship [that is, through His Lordship's continuous manifestations[10]], He alternates day and night like a white and a black thread, to inscribe His signs on the vast sheet of the universe. He is One, All-Majestic and Powerful, to Whom the sun, the moon, and the stars are all subjugated.

The palace's rooms are the thousands of worlds, each designed, furnished, and decorated in a specific way. The finest and most beautiful works of art are what we see here, each of which is a miracle of Divine Power; the food are the wonderful fruits of Divine Mercy that we see here, especially in summer; and the kitchen is the fire in the center of the earth and the heat of the sun. The precious stones are manifestations of the Divine Sacred Names, and the embellishments are the well-ordered, finely made beings and perfectly proportioned inscriptions of the Pen of the Power that adorn this world and point to the Names of the Majestic All-Powerful One.

The aide-de-camp is our master Prophet Muhammad. His assistants are all other Prophets, and his students are all saints and purified scholars. The servants are angels, the palace's inhabitants are humanity, and the invited guests are those animals created to serve humanity. The first group of people are believers, students of the Qur'an that interprets the verses of the Book of the Universe. The second group are the unbelievers and rebels, "deaf and dumb," misguided people who, obeying their carnal selves and Satan, accept only the worldly life and so place themselves below animals.

The first group, comprising the good and spiritually pros-
perous people, listened to the master's message of intellectual
enlightenment and spiritual well-being, the path of prosperity
in both worlds. This master is both a servant and a Messenger;
he is a worshipping servant on one hand in regard to his ser-
vanthood, who describes his Supreme Master and makes Him
known to people; an envoy of his community in the court of
Almighty God; and a Messenger on the other hand in regard to
his Messengership, who communicates his Master's commandments to humanity via the Qur'an.

In response to the Eternal King's declaration of His kingdom and His Oneness' manifestation throughout the universe,
they believed in and confirmed His Unity, and showed their
obedience and submission by saying: "We have heard and
obeyed." To the manifestation of the Divinity of the Lord of
the Worlds, they responded with worship by declaring that their
impotence was embedded in weakness, their poverty was embedded in need and the prescribed prayer (the essence of worship).

While in that huge mosque of the world, they devoted themselves to these and similar duties of worship and so assumed
the best pattern of creation. Above all other creatures, they became
God's trustworthy vicegerents, equipped with the blessing of
belief and trustworthiness.[11] After this trial and testing, and to
recompense their devotion to Islam, their Munificent Lord
rewarded their belief with eternal happiness and invited them
to the Abode of Peace. There, out of His Mercy, He bestowed on
them dazzling bounties beyond description and imagination,
and eternity and everlasting life. The observing and reflecting
lovers of an eternal, abiding beauty will go to eternity. Such is
the end and final station of those who study the Qur'an. May
Almighty God include us among them. Amen!

Members of the second group, all of them sinners and wicked people, entered the palace of this world at the age of discretion.[12] Disbelieving the evidence of Divine Oneness and ungrateful for the bounties, they insulted all creatures by accusing them of being worthless, and rejected and denied the manifestations of the Divine Names. In short, they committed a grave error in a short time and earned eternal punishment.

We have been given this capital of life and human faculties to spend on the duties mentioned above. Given this, our duty is not restricted to living an easy life and gratifying our carnal desires. Nor are our delicate senses and abilities, sensitive faculties and organs, well-ordered members and systems, and inquisitive senses and feelings included in the "machine" of our life (our body) to satisfy the base, carnal self's low desires. Rather, they were included therein and made a part of our nature for two reasons: first, to make us feel all varieties of the bounties bestowed by the Real Giver of Bounties, and to urge us to be grateful. So, feel them and be grateful to Him. The second reason was to make known and urge us to experience all manifestations of each Divine Sacred Name seen in the universe. So experience and know them, and believe. If we can realize these aims, we can gain human perfection and become true human beings.

> By the sun and its brightness, and the moon as it follows it, and the day as it reveals it, and the night as it enshrouds it, and the heaven and Him Who built it, and earth and Him Who spread it, and the soul and Him Who has formed it to perfection and inspired it (with conscience) of what is wrong for it and what is right for it. He is indeed prosperous who purifies it, and he has indeed failed who corrupts it. (Shams 91:1-10)

ISLAMIC VIEW OF MANKIND

GOD'S VICEGERENT ON EARTH

Behold, your Lord said to the angels: "I am setting on the earth a vicegerent." The angels asked: "Will you set therein one who will cause disorder and corruption on it and shed blood, while we glorify You with Your praise and declare that You alone are all-holy and to be worshipped as God and Lord." He said: "Surely I know what you do not know."

(God) taught Adam the names, all of them. Then (in order to clarify the supremacy of humankind and the wisdom in their being created and made vicegerent on the earth), He presented them (the things and beings, whose names had been taught to Adam, with their names) to the angels, and said, "Now tell Me the names of these, if you are truthful.

(The angels) said: "Glory be to You. We have no knowledge save what You have taught us. Surely You are the All-Knowing, the All-Wise."

(God) said: "O Adam, inform them of these things and beings with their names." When he (Adam) informed them with their names, He said (to the angels), "Did I not tell you that I know the unseen of the heavens and the earth, and I know all that you reveal and all that you have been concealing?"

And behold, We said to the angels: "Prostrate yourselves before Adam!" (Baqara 2:30-34)

ankind is superior to all other creation in the sense that God chose human beings as His vicegerent on earth. Adam was the first man and prophet, and he was superior to the angels as he was bestowed with the knowledge of the names of all things as well as being the reflection of all the Divine Names and Attributes. Mankind's superiority is not only indicated with Adam, but also confirmed with another verse in the Qur'an, *Surely We have created human of the best stature as the perfect pattern of creation* (Tin 95:4). Thus, in Islam people are not born into this world with an error that must be redeemed. Quite the opposite, humans embody many fine qualities like piety, generosity, and compassion, and people are expected to live up to this noble idea of humanity.

The quality of being human comes from our immaterial and spiritual aspects, not from our natural and material aspects. The spirit and intellect do not originate in the physical body; rather, the spirit uses the body, and only life gives the body any meaning.

We have three principal drives: desire, anger, and intellect. We desire or lust after the opposite sex, and love our children and worldly possessions. We direct our anger at what stands in our way, and by using it can defend ourselves. Our intellect enables us to make the right decisions. The Creator does not restrain these drives, but rather requires us to seek perfection through self-discipline so that we do not misuse them. If they remain undisciplined, immorality, illicit sexual relationships, and prohibited livelihoods, tyranny, injustice, deception, falsehood, and other vices will appear in individuals and throughout society. The above verse, *Surely We have created human of the best stature as the perfect pattern of creation*, is followed by, *Then We have reduced him to the lowest of the low, Except those who believe and do good, righteous deeds, so there is for them a reward constant and beyond measure.* This verse expresses the need for a heavenly discipline to save us from the *lowest of the low* for, despite its perfect pattern of creation, mankind is always face-to-face with the danger of failing this test of worldly life.

ALL HUMAN BEINGS ARE EQUAL

> O humankind! Surely We have created you from a single (pair of) male and female, and made you into tribes and families so that you may know one another (and so build mutuality and co-operative relationships, not so that you may take pride in your differences of race or social rank, and breed enmities). Surely the noblest, most honorable of you in God's sight is the one best in piety, righteousness, and reverence for God. Surely God is All-Knowing, All-Aware. (Hujurat 49:13)

As clearly seen in the above verse, the Islamic view of mankind is egalitarian and does not condone any discrimination based on gender, race, color, family, socio-economic standing, culture, or nation. The only criterion for superiority is "piety, righteousness, and reverence for God," and this can truly be known only by God. All humans are the offspring of Adam and Eve, and in this sense, we are all brothers and sisters.

Racism is one of the most severe problems of our age. When God's Messenger, peace and blessings be upon him, was raised as a Prophet, the attitudes behind racism were prevalent in Mecca in the guise of tribalism. The Quraysh considered themselves (in particular) and Arabs (in general) as being superior to all other people. God's Messenger came with this Divine message and proclaimed: *"No Arab is superior to a non-Arab, and no white person is superior to a black person"*[13]; and *"If a black Abyssinian Muslim is to rule over Muslims, he should be obeyed."*[14]

God's Messenger eradicated color-based racism and discrimination so successfully that, for example, Umar once said of Bilal, who was black: "Bilal is our master, and was emancipated by our master Abu Bakr."[15] Once Abu Dharr got so angry with Bilal that he insulted him: "You son of a black woman!" Bilal came to God's Messenger and reported the incident in tears. The Messenger reproached Abu Dharr: "Do you still have a sign of Ignorance?" Full of repentance, Abu Dharr lay on the ground and said: "I won't raise my head (meaning he would-n't get up) unless Bilal puts his foot on it to pass over it." Bilal forgave him, and they were reconciled.[16] Zayd ibn Harithah, a black slave emancipated by God's Messenger, was his adopted son before the Revelation banned such adoptions. The Prophet married him to Zaynab bint Jahsh, one of the noblest (and non-black) Arab and Muslim women. In addition, he chose Zayd as the commander of the Muslim army that was sent against the Byzantine Empire, even though it included such leading Companions as Abu Bakr, Umar, Ja'far ibn Abi Talib (the cousin of God's Messenger), and Khalid ibn Walid (even then, famed for his genius as a military commander).[17] The Prophet appointed Zayd's son, Usamah, to command the army he formed just before his death. Included therein were such leading Companions as Abu Bakr, Umar, Khalid, Abu Ubaydah, Talhah, and Zubayr. This established in the Muslims' hearts and minds that supe-riority is not by birth or color or blood, but by righteousness and devotion to God.

In Islam, all human beings are granted equal access to God. There is not a specific class of priesthood, nor has any privi-lege been promised to any group of people. All believers are equal servants of God, and thus need no mediator.

Islam is not for one family or nation; it is not a covenant made with a chosen group. Islam encompasses all of humani-ty and even the smallest of creatures.

THE PROPHET MUHAMMAD

I f we were to imagine ourselves in the world 1,400 years ago, we would find a completely different place. The opportunity to exchange ideas would be sparse, and the means of communication limited and undeveloped. Darkness would hold sway, and only a faint glimmer of learning, hardly enough to illuminate the horizon of human knowledge, would be visible. The people of that time had a narrow outlook, and their ideas of humanity and the world were confined to their limited surroundings. Steeped in ignorance and superstition, their unbelief was so strong and widespread that they refused to accept anything as lofty or sublime unless it appeared in the garb of the supernatural. They had developed such an inferiority complex that they could not imagine any person having a godly soul or a saintly disposition.

THE PROPHET'S HOMELAND

In that benighted era, darkness lay heavier and thicker in one land than in any other. The neighboring countries of Persia, Byzantium, and Egypt possessed a glimmer of civilization and a faint light of learning, but the Arabian peninsula, isolated and cut off by vast oceans of sand, was culturally and intellectually one of the world's most backward areas. The Hejaz, the birthplace of the Prophet, peace and blessings be upon him, had not reached even the limited development of neighboring regions, and had not experienced any social evolution or attained any intellectual development of note. Although the highly developed language of the region could express the finest shades of meaning, a study of their literature's remnants reveals the limited extent of their knowledge. All of this illustrates their limited cultural and standards of civilization, their deeply superstitious nature, their barbarous and ferocious customs, and their uncouth and degraded moral standards and conceptions.

It was a land without a government, for every tribe claimed sovereignty and considered itself independent. The only law recognized was that of the "jungle." Robbery, arson, and the murder of innocent and weak people were the norm. Life, property, and honor were constantly at risk, and tribes were always at daggers drawn with each other. A trivial incident could engulf them in ferocious warfare, which sometimes developed into a decades-long and countrywide conflagration. As one scholar writes:

> These struggles destroyed the sense of national unity and developed an incurable particularism; each tribe deeming itself self-sufficient and regarding the rest as its legitimate victims for murder, robbery and plunder.[18]

Barely able to discriminate between pure and impure, lawful and unlawful, their concepts of morals, culture, and civilization were primitive and uncouth. Their life was wild and their behavior was barbaric. They reveled in adultery, gambling, and drinking. They stood naked before each other without shame, and women circumambulated the Ka'ba, the holy shrine, in the nude.

Their prestige called for female infanticide. Worshippers of stones, trees, idols, stars, and spirits, they had forgotten the earlier prophets' teachings. They had an idea that Abraham and Ishmael were their forefathers, but almost all of these forefathers' religious knowledge and understanding of God had been lost.

MUHAMMAD'S LIFE BEFORE HIS PROPHETHOOD

This was the Prophet Muhammad's homeland where he was born in 571. His father, Abdullah, died before he was born, and his mother, Amina, died when he was 6 years old. Consequently, he was deprived of whatever training and upbringing an Arab child of that time received. During his childhood, he tended flocks of sheep and goats with other Bedouin boys. As education never touched him, he remained completely unlettered and unschooled.

The Prophet left the Arabian Peninsula only twice. As a youth, he accompanied his uncle Abu Talib on a trade mission to al-Sham (present-day Israel, Palestine, Lebanon, Syria, and Jordan). The other time was when he led another trade mission to the same region for the widow Khadija, a wealthy Meccan merchant 15 years his senior. They got married when he was 25, and lived happily together until she died, more than 20 years later.

Being unlettered, he read no Jewish or Christian religious texts or had any appreciable relationship with them. Mecca's ideas and customs were idolatrous and wholly untouched by Christian or Jewish religious thought. Even Mecca's *hanifs*, those who followed some of Abraham's pure religion in an adulterated and unclear form and rejected idolatry, were not influenced by Judaism or Christianity. No Jewish or Christian thought is reflected in these people's surviving poetic heritage. Had the Prophet made any effort to become acquainted with their thought, it would have been noticed.

Moreover, Muhammad, peace and blessings be upon him, avoided the locally popular intellectual forms of poetry and rhetoric even before his prophethood. History records no distinction that set him over others, except for his moral commitment, trustworthiness, honesty, truthfulness, and integrity. He did not lie, an assertion proven by the fact that not even his worst enemies ever called him a liar. He talked politely and never used obscene or abusive language. His charming personality and excellent manners captivated the hearts of those who met him. He always followed the principles of justice, altruism, and fair play with others, and never deceived anyone or broke his promise.

Muhammad, peace and blessings be upon him, was engaged in trade and commerce for years, but never entered into a dishonest transaction. Those who had business dealings with him had full confidence in his integrity. Everyone called him *al-Amin* ("the truthful and the trustworthy"). Everyone could leave their precious belongings with him for safe custody, and he scrupulously fulfilled their trusts. In sum, he was the embodiment of modesty in society that was immodest to the core.

Born and raised among people who regarded drunkenness and gambling as virtues, he never drank alcohol nor gambled. He helped orphans, widows, and the poor, and was hospitable to travelers. Harming no one, he exposed himself to hardship for their sake. Avoiding tribal feuds, he was the foremost worker for reconciliation. He never bowed before any created thing or partook of offerings made to idols, even when he was a child, for he hated all worship devoted to that which was not God. In brief, his towering and radiant personality, when placed in the midst of such a benighted and dark environment, may be likened to a beacon of light illumining a pitch-dark night, to a diamond shining among a heap of stones.

MISSION

In the year 610 a remarkable change came over him when he was 40. His heart, illuminated with Divine Light, now had the strength for which he had yearned. During one of his many retreats to Mount Hira for reflection during the month of Ramadan, he received the first Revelation from the Archangel Gabriel (Jibril). Gabriel said to Muhammad, "Read." Muhammad replied, "I cannot read," as he had received no formal education and was unlettered. Gabriel then embraced him until he reached the limit of his endurance and, after releasing him, said, "Read." Muhammad's answer was the same as before. Gabriel repeated the embrace for the third time, asked him to repeat after him and said:

> Read in the name of your Lord who created! He created humanity from that which clings. Read; and your Lord is most Bountiful, He who has taught by the pen, taught humanity what it knew not. (Alaq 96:1-5)

That day, Muhammad was granted his mission as the final Prophet; thus, he left the confinement of the cave to which he used to retire at regular intervals, went to his people, and invited them to Islam.

MUHAMMAD AS A MESSENGER OF GOD

For 40 years, Muhammad lived as an ordinary man among his people. He was not known as a statesman, preacher, or orator. No one had heard him impart wisdom and knowledge, nor discuss principles of metaphysics, ethics, law, politics, economy, or sociology. He had no reputation as a soldier, nor any noted potential for being a great general. He had said nothing about God, angels, revealed Books, early Prophets, bygone nations, the

Day of Judgment, life after death, or Heaven and Hell. No doubt he had an excellent character and charming manners and was well-behaved, yet nothing marked him out as one who would accomplish something great and revolutionary. His acquaintances knew him as a sober, calm, gentle, and trustworthy citizen of good nature. But when he left the Hira cave with a new message, he was completely transformed.

When he began preaching, his people stood in awe and wonder, bedazzled by his eloquence and oratory. It was so impressive and captivating that even his worst enemies were afraid to listen to it, lest it penetrate their hearts or very being and make them abandon their traditional religion and culture. It was so beyond compare that no Arab poet, preacher, or orator, no matter how gifted, could equal its beautiful language and splendid diction when challenged to do so. Although they put their heads together, they could not produce even one line like the ones he recited.

Facing immediate and severe opposition, he confronted his opponents with a smile and remained undeterred by their criticism and coercion. When the people realized that their threats did not frighten this noble man and that the severest tribulations directed toward him and his followers had no effect, they resorted to another tactic—but that, too, was destined to fail.

A deputation of the leading members of the Quraysh (his tribe) offered him a bribe to abandon his mission:

> If you want wealth, we will amass for you as much as you wish; if you want honor and power, we will swear allegiance to you as our overlord and king; if you want beauty, you shall have the hand of the most beautiful maiden of your choice.

The terms were extremely tempting for any ordinary person, but they had no significance in the Prophet's eyes. His reply fell like a bomb upon the deputation, who thought they had played their trump card:

> I want neither wealth nor power. God has commissioned me to warn humanity. I deliver His message to you. If you accept it, you shall have felicity and joy in this life and eternal bliss in the life hereafter. If you reject it, God will decide between you and me.

On another occasion, he said to his uncle, who was being pressured by the tribal leaders to persuade him to abandon his mission:

> O uncle! Should they place the sun in my right hand and the moon in my left so as to make me renounce this mission, I shall not do so. I will never give it up. Either it will please God to make it triumph or I shall perish in the attempt.[19]

The faith, perseverance, and resolution with which he conducted his mission to ultimate success are eloquent proof of the supreme truth of his cause. Had there been the slightest doubt or uncertainty in his heart, he would never have been able to brave the storm that continued in all its fury for 23 long years.

COMMITMENT TO THE CALL

The first people to accept the Prophet's invitation to Islam were Khadija, Ali, Zayd ibn Haritha and Abu Bakr. They were followed by Uthman, Abdurrahman ibn Awf, Sa'd ibn Abi Waqqas, Talha and Zubayr. Those first Muslims, in particular the Prophet, underwent great torment at the hands of the idol worshippers. In fact, many Muslims, like Yasir and his wife, Sumayya, were murdered after unbearable torture.

The resistance of these first Muslims greatly affected the spread of Islam. As a matter of fact, during the first six years of his prophethood, strong and brave men like Hamza and Umar embraced Islam and found their place among the Companions of the Prophet. As the number of those who believed in Islam increased, so did the number of obstacles placed by the pagans to prevent the spread of this new faith. In the fifth and sixth year of prophethood, some Muslims were forced by the situation to attain permission from the Prophet to emigrate to Abyssinia.

In the seventh year, the unbelievers isolated the Muslims in one area and boycotted them. They were banned from trade, travel, and interrelations with other people. This situation lasted for three years. In the tenth year of the prophethood, with the successive deaths of Khadija and Abu Talib, the torment and suffering caused by the enemies of Islam increased yet again. Khadija and Abu Talib were respected people in the community and this respect had, to some extent, provided a degree of protection for the Prophet.

The Prophet went to Taif to try to gain some outside support. But the people of Taif not only did not accept Islam or give support to the Prophet, they stoned him, and he was only able to save himself only by sheltering in an orchard outside Taif, covered in his own blood. In his supplication, after having undergone this horrible treatment, the Prophet said that if he were truly fulfilling his mission, then such torture meant nothing to him. It is without a doubt that he acted correctly and that he fulfilled his responsibilities.

Despite all the difficulties, Prophet Muhammad's efforts to spread the message of Islam continued. He intensified most of his efforts on the crossroads where travelers from outside the city might pass. Finally, a group of six people who had come from Medina (then Yathrib) for pilgrimage testified the truth of the message he brought and promised to fulfill the conditions of Islam. The following year, five of this group came together with seven other people from Medina and gave their pledge to the Prophet at Aqaba. A second pledge took place with seventy-five people the next year, who promised to protect the Prophet as they protected their own women and children. In the time that followed this, with the permission of God and that of the Prophet, the Muslims who were suffering in Mecca emigrated from there to Medina. This is known as the *Hijra* in Islamic literature, and marks the start of the Islamic calendar. The last to emigrate were the Prophet and Abu Bakr. This was a very difficult emigration, with the pagans of Mecca chasing them from the Thawr caves to the south of Mecca, and continuing pursuit until they had almost reached Medina. The Prophet and Abu Bakr traveled in great danger, but in the end, they managed to reach Medina. The Medinan people, in contrast to the Meccans, took the Prophet to their bosoms. They united around him. They supported those who had abandoned their homes in Mecca for the glory of God. It is for this reason that Almighty God calls the people of Medina the *Ansar* (the helpers) in the Qur'an. As a matter of fact, brotherhood and sisterhood was established between the emigrants and the *Ansar* immediately after the emigration of the Prophet. In this way, the action of helping people gained a spiritual dimension. This support helped to waylay psychological problems. The emigrants found the opportunity to share their experience of Islam with the people of Medina. The emigrants established shops and markets, and they were able to support themselves in a very short time. In this way, the Muslims benefited the economic life of the city.

These developments frightened the pagans in Mecca. They wanted to destroy the Muslims before they became any stronger. The result was battles between the Muslims and the pagans, like Badr, Uhud, the Battle of the Trench, and Muraysi. In the year 630, Mecca was conquered. The Prophet returned in triumph to the city from which he had been driven. The purpose behind this return was to cleanse the Ka'ba and the surrounding area of idols, and return it to its original state as it had been when built by Adam and then re-built by the Prophet Abraham. The Prophet did not act in revenge; he did not act with resentment. Rather, he issued a general pardon. He showed his greatness by forgiving when he was strong. He was planning unification, a celebration, and he had no time to waste on trivial matters. As a matter of fact, the muezzin of the Prophet, Bilal al-Habashi, by calling noon prayer from the roof of the Ka'ba, announced the superiority of unity and of one God to the skies of Mecca.

The proud and haughty tribe of Hawazin, who could not stomach these new developments, laid plans to prevent the development of the Muslims; but these plans were unsuccessful. They were defeated in their war against the Muslims. As a result, Islam resounded throughout the region, starting from the Hejaz region, and stretching throughout the Arabian Peninsula. Within one year after the Prophet had returned to Medina, he hosted the representatives from hundreds of tribes.

In 632, during the time of the Hajj, the Prophet spoke before more than one hundred thousand Muslims. Known as the Farewell Sermon, this speech was a summary of Islamic thought and presented the most perfect principles in human rights. The beloved Prophet, who was able to communicate the message entrusted to him thanks to his patience, determination, and bravery, closed his eyes to this world on June 8, 632, a Monday.

WHAT WAS HIS MESSAGE?

The Prophet Muhammad is defined in the Qur'an as *a giver of glad tidings* and *a warner*. When he returned his community with his mission, he challenged the corrupt status quo as well as the distorted forms of belief. What he preached to his society and peoples of all times can be briefly versed as follows

> The idols that you worship are mere shams, so stop worshipping them. No person, star, tree, stone, or spirit deserves your worship. Do not bow your heads before them in worship. The entire universe belongs to God Almighty. He alone is the Creator, Nourisher, Sustainer, and thus the real Sovereign before Whom all should bow down and Who is worthy of your prayers and obedience. So worship Him alone and obey His commands.
>
> The theft and plunder, murder and rape, injustice and cruelty, and all the vices in which you indulge, are sins in God's eyes. Leave your evil ways. Speak the truth. Be just. Do not kill anyone, for whoever kills a person unjustly is like one who has killed all humanity, and whoever saves a person's life is like one who has saved all humanity (5:32). Do not rob anyone, but take your lawful share and give that which is due to others in a just manner.
>
> Do not set up other deities with God, or you will be condemned and forsaken. If one or both of your parents reaches old age and lives with you, speak to them only with respect and, out of mercy, be humble before them. Give your relatives their due. Give to the needy and the traveler, and do not be wasteful. Do not kill your children because you fear poverty or for other reasons. Shun adultery, for it is indecent and evil. Leave the property of orphans and the weak intact.

Fulfill the covenant, because you will be questioned about it. Do not cheat when you measure and weigh items. Do not pursue that of which you have no knowledge, for your ears, eyes, and heart will be questioned about this. Do not walk around arrogantly, for you will never tear the earth open or attain the mountains in height. Speak kind words to each other, for Satan uses strong words to cause strife. Do not turn your cheek in scorn and anger toward others or walk with impudence in the land.

God does not love those who boast, so be modest in bearing and subdue your voice. Do not make fun of others, for they may be better than you. Do not find fault with each other or call each other by offensive nicknames. Avoid most suspicion, for some suspicion is a sin. Do not spy on or gossip about each other. Be staunch followers of justice and witnesses for God, even though it be against yourselves, or your parents and relatives, regardless if they are rich or poor. Do not deviate by following caprice. Be steadfast witnesses for God in equity, and do not let your hatred of others seduce you to be unjust toward them.

Restrain your rage and pardon the offences of others. Good and evil deeds are not alike. Repel the evil deed with a good one. The recompense for an intentional evil is a similar evil; but whoever pardons and amends the evildoer with kindness and love will be rewarded by God. Avoid alcohol and games of chance, for God has forbidden them.

You are human beings, and all human beings are equal in God's eyes. No one is born with the slur of shame on his or her face or the mantle of honor around his or her neck. The only high and honored people are the God-conscious and pious, true in words and deeds. Distinctions of birth and glory of race are no criteria of greatness and honor.

On a day after you die, you will appear before a Supreme Court and account for all your deeds, none of which can be hidden. Your life's record shall be an open book to God. Your fate shall be determined by your good or bad actions.

In the court of the True Judge—the Omniscient God—there can be no unfair recommendation and favoritism. You cannot bribe Him, and your pedigree or parentage will be ignored. True faith and good deeds alone will benefit you at that time. Those who have done them fully shall reside in the Heaven of eternal happiness, while those who did not shall reside in the fire of Hell.[20]

THE QUR'AN

The Qur'an consists of the rhythmic verses, phrases, sentences, and chapters relayed by the Prophet as they were revealed to him by God, and which he proclaimed as the everlasting miracle testifying to his prophethood. He challenged the Arabs of his time who doubted its Divine origin, as well as all unbelieving Arabs and non-Arabs who would come later.

EARLIER DIVINE REVELATIONS AND THE QUR'AN

Another essential of Islamic faith is believing in all the Divine Books God sent to His different Messengers throughout history. God revealed His Books to His Prophets before Prophet Muhammad in exactly the same way. God informs us in the Qur'an of some of them: the Pages of Abraham, the Torah, the Zabur (the Psalms), and the Injil (the Gospel). We do not know the names of the books given to other Prophets, and therefore cannot say with certainty whether they were originally revealed books or not.

These earlier Divine Books were sent down in now-dead languages that only a few people today claim to understand. Given this, even if these books still existed in their original and unadulterated forms, it would be virtually impossible to understand them correctly and to interpret and implement their injunctions. Furthermore, as the original texts of most of these earlier Divine Books have been lost with the passage of time, only their translations exist today. The Qur'an, on the other hand, exists in its original language, which is still spoken and understood by millions of people.

DEFINING THE QUR'AN AND SOME OF ITS ATTRIBUTES

The general definition of the Qur'an is as follows: The Qur'an is the miraculous Word of God revealed to the Prophet Muhammad, written down and transmitted to succeeding generations by many reliable channels, and whose recitation is an act of worship and obligatory in daily prayers.

The Qur'an describes some of its features as follows:

> The month of Ramadan (is the month) in which the Qur'an was sent down as a guidance for humanity and clear proofs of the Guidance and the Criterion. (Baqara 2:185)

> This Qur'an could not have been invented (by anyone) apart from God, but confirms what was (revealed) before it, a fuller explanation of the Book—wherein there is no doubt—from the Lord of the Worlds. (Yunus 10:37)

> We have sent it as an Arabic Qur'an that you may understand and use your reason. (Yusuf 12:2)

> This Qur'an guides to that which is most right, and gives good tidings to believers who do deeds of righteousness, that theirs will be a great reward. (Isra 17:9)

> And in truth We have made the Qur'an easy to reflect and take lesson, but will any take heed? (Qamar 54:17)

> That this is a noble Qur'an, in a hidden, guarded Book. (Waqia 56:77-78)

The Qur'an has other titles, each of which describes one of its aspects and thus can be regarded as one of its attributes, such as: the Book, the Criterion, the Remembrance, the Advice, the Light, the Guidance, the Healer, the Noble, the Book in Pairs, the Mother of the Book, the Truth, the Admonishment, the Good Tiding, the Book Gradually Revealed, the Knowledge, and the Clear. Concerning the Qur'an, the Prophet Muhammad says:

> The Qur'an distinguishes between truth and falsehood. It is not for entertainment, for those who reject it will be punished. It contains the history of previous peoples and tidings of those who will come later, and rules on people's disagreements. Those who look elsewhere for guidance are led astray by God. It is God's strong rope, the wise instruction, and the Straight Path. It is a book that desires cannot deviate or tongues confuse, one that does not bore scholars or wear them out due to repetition, and one possessing uncountable admirable aspects. All who hear it say: "We heard a wonderful Qur'an guiding to righteousness, and so we believe in it." Those who base their words on it speak truly. Whoever judges by it judges justly, and whoever calls to it calls to truth.[21]

Arabic, the language of revelation, is the Qur'an's outer body. Religion does not consist only of philosophy or theology, but is a method of unifying all dimensions of our being. Therefore, Arabic is an essential, inseparable element of the Qur'an.

The Qur'an views the world as the cradle of brotherhood and sisterhood. It seeks to unite all races, colors, and beliefs as brothers and sisters and servants of the One God. Its language is a basic factor that helps people contemplate religious realities and unite all dimensions of their being according to divine standards. Translations cannot be recited in prescribed prayers, for no translation is identical with the original Arabic.

The Qur'an is the source of all knowledge in Islam, be it religious, spiritual, social, scientific, moral, legal, or philosophical. As the guide to all truth, it has four main purposes:

a) to show God's Existence and Unity,

b) to establish prophethood and the afterlife,

c) to promulgate the worship of God,

d) to set forth the essentials of justice.

Its verses mainly dwell upon these purposes, and thus contain creedal principles, rules governing human life, detailed information on the Resurrection and the afterlife, how to worship God, morality, direct or indirect information on some scientific facts, principles of civil formation and decay, historical outlines of previous civilizations, and so on.

The Qur'an is a source of healing, as applying it in daily life cures almost all psychological and social illnesses, as well as a cosmology, epistemology, ontology, sociology, psychology, and law revealed to regulate human life for all people, regardless of time or place. In fact, the Prophet declares: "The Qur'an is more lovable to God than the heavens and earth and those in them."[22]

ARGUMENTS FOR THE QUR'AN'S DIVINE AUTHORSHIP

- Eloquence, poetry, and oratory enjoyed great prestige in pre-Islamic Arabia. Poetry competitions were held regularly, and winning poems were written in gold and hung on the walls of the Ka'ba. The Prophet had never been heard to say even a couple lines of poetry. However, the Qur'an he brought eventually forced all known experts to surrender.

- Even the unbelievers were captivated by it. Nevertheless, to stop Islam from spreading, they said it was magical and should not be heeded. But when prominent pre-Islamic poets such as Khansa and Labid converted and then abandoned poetry out of respect for and awe of the styles and eloquence of the Qur'an, the unbelievers had to confess: "If we call it a piece of poetry, it is not. If we designate it a piece of rhymed prose, it is not. If we describe it as the word of a soothsayer, it is not."[23] At times, they could not help listening to the Prophet's recitation secretly at night, but they could not overcome their arrogance long enough to believe in its divine origin.

• No one, regardless of intelligence, can establish rules to solve all potential problems. Even the best system must be revised at least every 50 years. More importantly, no system can promise eternal happiness, for its principles are restricted to this transient human life that is infinitely short when compared to the afterlife. In contrast, no Qur'anic principle has become obsolete or needs revision. For example, it states that wealth should not circulate only among the rich (Hashr 59:7); that government offices should be entrusted to competent, qualified persons, and that absolute justice should be the rule in public administration and all disputes (Nisa 4:58); that people can have only that for which they strive (Najm 53:39); and that whoever kills a person unjustly is the same as one who would kill all humanity (Maidah 5:32). These and many other principles (e.g., prohibiting usury, gambling, alcohol, and extramarital sexual relations; enjoining prayer, fasting, alms-giving, and good conduct), are strengthened through love and awareness of God, the promise of an eternal happy life, and the fear of punishment in Hell.

• The Qur'an also unveils the mystery of humanity, creation, and the universe. The Qur'an, humanity, and the universe are the three "books" that make the Creator known to us, and are three expressions of the same truth. Therefore, the One Who created humanity and the universe also revealed the Qur'an.

• The Prophet was very austere and shunned worldly gain, fame, political power, wealth, and carnal desires. Also, he endured great hardship and persecution. To claim that he invented the Qur'an means that Muhammad the Trustworthy, as he was commonly known, was the greatest liar and cheat history has ever known. Why would he falsely claim prophethood and expose himself and his family to such severe deprivation and persecution? Such accusations, as well as that of saying that he wrote the Qur'an, are totally groundless and lacking in evidence.

RECORDING AND PRESERVING THE QUR'AN

> Without doubt, We sent down the Message and We will preserve it (Hijr 15:9)

The name of the religion that God Almighty revealed through all messengers is Islam. Just as the laws ordering and operating the universe remain the same and constant, and just as all people have the same basic characteristics, essential needs, and final destination, regardless of when and where they live, it is natural for religion to be based upon the same essentials of belief, worship, and morality.

Muhammad was sent as the last Messenger and with the perfected form of the divine religion (Islam). God protects this final and perfected religion by promising to preserve the Qur'an. People who followed the messages brought by Moses and later by Jesus called their faiths Judaism and Christianity, respectively, whereas Islam has retained its original and God-given name.

In this world, as God Almighty acts behind natural or material causes, He is also behind the causes or means of preserving the Qur'an. One of these is having the Qur'an written down during the Prophet's lifetime and under his direct supervision so that nothing could be deleted, added, or changed. All copies of the Qur'an that have existed during the 14 centuries of Islam are exactly the same. Unlike other earlier scriptures, the Qur'an has been preserved in its original form or text and in the language in which it was revealed. Thus the following points are of considerable significance:

The Qur'an was revealed in parts. God Almighty undertook its preservation, due recitation, and the arrangement of its parts. He revealed to His Messenger where each revealed verse and chapter was to be placed:

> Do not move your tongue (with the revelation) so that you may hasten (committing) it (to memory). It is for Us to collect it and to promulgate it. But when We have promulgated it, follow its recital (as promulgated). Then it is also for us to explain it. (Qiyama 75:16-19)

> High above all (considerations) is God, the Sovereign, the Truth. Do not show haste to receive and recite the Qur'an before its revelation to you is completed; but rather say: "Lord, increase me in knowledge." (Ta-Ha 20:114)

The Almighty emphasizes that no falsehood can touch the Qur'an or cast doubt upon its authenticity:

> These are the people who rejected the Message when it came to them. But the fact is that this is a noble, mighty Book. No falsehood can approach it from before or behind. It is a Revelation being sent down from One All-Wise, All-Praised. (Fussilat 41:41-42)

Once a year, the Messenger reviewed all that had been revealed up to that point with Archangel Gabriel. In his last year, after the Revelation was completed, Gabriel came twice for this purpose. The Messenger concluded from this that he would die soon.

From the very beginning, the Companions paid the utmost attention to the Qur'an and tried their best to understand, memorize, and learn it. In fact, the Qur'an ordered them to do so: *When the Qur'an is recited, give ear to it and pay heed, that you may obtain mercy* (Araf 7:204).

The Qur'an was revealed piecemeal and mostly on specific occasions. Whenever a verse, chapter, or group of verses was revealed, it was memorized by many Companions and written down by scribes who had been chosen by the Prophet specifically for that purpose. The Messenger also told them where to place the new verse in the Qur'an. Known as the Scribes of the Revelation, these 40 or so Companions also copied the pieces for themselves and preserved them.[24]

The Almighty declares: *It is for Us to collect it and to promulgate it* (Qiyama 75:17). The verses and chapters of the Qur'an were arranged and collected according to the Prophet's instructions [while he was still alive], which were guided by revelation. The official version was formed after the Battle of Yamama. When a disagreement appeared over the pronunciation of certain words, the formal version was copied and sent to important centers during the reign of Caliph Uthman ibn Affan (644-56).[25]

One of the foremost reasons why the Qur'an has remained uncorrupted is that it has been preserved in its original language. No one in the Muslim world has ever thought to supplant or replace it with a translation, and so it was never exposed to imprecise or mistaken translations, or to additions or deletions.

In conclusion, the Qur'an that we hold in our hands today is the same Qur'an that the Prophet received from God. Its authenticity and genuineness is without doubt. No Muslim scholar of any standard has ever doubted this, and none have questioned that the Prophet spoke every word that we find in the Qur'an today.

ISLAMIC CIVILIZATION

During the Middle Ages (known as the Dark Ages in European history) a magnificent civilization was flourishing in the Muslim East. Obeying the Qur'anic injunctions, Muslims studied the Book of Divine Revelation (the Qur'an) and the Book of Creation (the universe) and established the most magnificent civilization of human history. Scholars from all over the old world benefited from the centers of higher learning at Damascus, Bukhara, Baghdad, Cairo, Fez, Qairawan, Zeitona, Cordoba, Sicily, Isfahan, Delhi, and elsewhere throughout the Muslim world. Historians liken the Muslim world of that time to a beehive, for roads were full of students, scientists, and scholars traveling from one center of learning to another. Such world-renowned figures as al-Kindi, al-Khwarizmi, al-Farabi, Ibn Sina, al-Mas'udi, Ibn al-Haytham, al-Biruni, al-Ghazzali, Nasir al-Din al-Tusi, al-Zahrawi and many others shone like stars in the firmament of the sciences.

In his multi-volume *Introduction to the History of Science* (1927-48), George Sarton divided his work into 50-year periods, naming each chapter after that period's most eminent scientist. From the middle of the eighth century to the twelfth century AD, each of the seven 50-year periods carries the name of a Muslim scientist: "the Time of al-Khwarizmi," "the Time of al-Biruni," and so on. Within these chapters, Sarton lists 100 important Muslim scientists and their principal works. Likewise, John Davenport, a leading scientist, observed:

> It must be owned that all the knowledge whether of Physics, Astronomy, Philosophy or Mathematics, which flourished

in Europe from the 10th century was originally derived from
the Arabian schools, and the Spanish Saracen may be looked
upon as the father of European philosophy.[26]

Bertrand Russell, the famous British philosopher, wrote:

> The supremacy of the East was not only military. Science,
> philosophy, poetry, and the arts, all flourished in the Mo-
> hammedan world at a time when Europe was sunk in barba-
> rism. Europeans, with unpardonable insularity, call this per-
> iod "the Dark Ages": but it was only in Europe that it was
> dark—indeed only in Christian Europe, for Spain, which was
> Mohammedan, had a brilliant culture.[27]

Robert Briffault, the renowned historian, acknowledges in
his *The Making of Humanity*:

> It is highly probable that but for the Arabs, modern Euro-
> pean civilization would have never assumed that character
> which has enabled it to transcend all previous phases of evo-
> lution. For although there is not a single aspect of human
> growth in which the decisive influence of Islamic culture is
> not traceable, nowhere is it so clear and momentous as in the
> genesis of that power which constitutes the paramount dis-
> tinctive force of the modern world and the supreme course
> of its victory—natural sciences and the scientific spirit...
> What we call sciences arose in Europe as a result of a new
> spirit of inquiry; of new methods of investigation, of the me-
> thod of experiment, observation, measurement, of the deve-
> lopment of Mathematics in a form unknown to the Greeks.
> That spirit and those methods were introduced into the Eu-
> ropean world by the Arabs.[28]

L. Stoddard acknowledges that for its first five centuries, the
realm of Islam was the most civilized and progressive portion
of the world. Studded with splendid cities, gracious mosques,
and quiet universities, the Muslim East offered a striking contrast to the West, which was sunk in the night of the Dark Ages.[29]

This bright civilization progressed until it suffered terrible disasters coming like huge overlapping waves: the European Crusades (1097-1270) and the Mongol Invasion (1216-58). These disasters continued for centuries, until the Muslim government in Baghdad collapsed (1258) and the history of Islam entered a new phase in the thirteenth century with the Ottoman Turks. Islamic civilization was still vigorous and remained far ahead of the world in economic and military fields until the eighteenth century, despite (from the sixteenth century onward) losing ground in the sciences.

In the tenth century, Muslim Cordoba was Europe's most civilized city, the wonder and admiration of the world. Travelers from the north heard of the city that contained 70 libraries, with hundreds of thousands of volumes, and 900 public baths. Whenever the rulers of Leon, Navarre, or Barcelona needed a surgeon, architect, dressmaker, or musician, they contacted Cordoba.[30] Muslim literary prestige was so great in Spain that the Bible and the liturgy had to be translated into Arabic for the indigenous Christian community. The account given by Alvaro, a zealous Christian writer, shows vividly how even non-Muslim Spaniards were attracted to Arab/Muslim literature:

> My fellow Christians delight in the poems and romances of the Arabs. They study the works of Muhammadan theologians and philosophers, not in order to refute them, but to acquire a correct and elegant Arabic style. Where today can a layman be found who reads the Latin commentaries on holy Scriptures? Who is there that studies the Gospels, the Prophets, the Apostles? Alas, the young Christians who are the most conspicuous for their talents have no knowledge of any literature or language save the Arabic; they read and study with avidity Arabian books; they amass whole libraries of them at a vast cost, and they everywhere sing the praises of the Arabian world.[31]

If the purpose of education and civilization is to raise people's pride, dignity, and honor so that they can improve their state and consequently the state of society, Islamic civilization has proven its value. Many writers have discussed Islam's ability to transform the societies with which it comes into contact. For example, in his speech about Islam's effects and influence upon people, delivered at the Church Congress of England, Isaac Taylor said:

> When Muhammadanism is embraced, paganism, fetishism, infanticide and witchcraft disappear. Filth is replaced by cleanliness and the new convert acquires personal dignity and self-respect. Immodest dances and promiscuous intercourse of the sexes cease; female chastity is rewarded as a virtue; industry replaces idleness; license gives place to law; order and sobriety prevail; blood feuds, cruelty to animals and slaves are eradicated. Islam swept away corruption and superstitions. Islam was a revolt against empty polemics. It gave hope to the slave, brotherhood to mankind, and recognition to the fundamental facts of human nature. The virtues which Islam inculcates are temperance, cleanliness, chastity, justice, fortitude, courage, benevolence, hospitality, veracity and resignation ... Islam preaches a practical brotherhood, the social equality of all Muslims. Slavery is not part of the creed of Islam. Polygamy is a more difficult question. Moses did not prohibit it. It was practiced by David and it is not directly forbidden in the New Testament. Muhammad limited the unbounded license of polygamy. It is the exception rather than the rule ... In resignation to God's Will, temperance, chastity, veracity and in brotherhood of believers they (the Muslims) set us a pattern which we should do well to follow. Islam has abolished drunkenness, gambling and prostitution, the three curses of the Christian lands. Islam has done more for civilization than Christianity. The conquest of one-third of the earth to his (Muhammad's) creed was a miracle.[32]

Belief – Six Pillars

- ➤ One True God
- ➤ Angels
- ➤ Books – Divine Scriptures
- ➤ Prophets
- ➤ Day of Judgment – Accountability
- ➤ Divine Decree

The Messenger believes in what has been sent down to him from his Lord, and so do the believers; each one believes in God, and His angels, and His Books, and His Messengers: "We make no distinction between any of His Messengers (in believing in them)." And they say: "We have heard and obeyed. Our Lord, grant us Your forgiveness, and to You is the homecoming." (Baqara 2:285)

Belief, iman in Arabic, is to assert with one's intellect and conviction of the heart that there is no God but God, and Muhammad is His Messenger. Belief further includes believing that there is an eternal life after this world and that all humanity will be tried on the Day of Judgment; that angels exist and act as servants of God; that there is a Divine Decree and Destiny in operation together with human free-will.

Belief is submission to One Supreme Being, God Almighty, and freeing oneself from submission to one's carnal self. It is a conviction that the cosmos is not an end product of accidental natural phenomena, but a direct sign which points to the Creator. Belief entails an intellectual capacity to "reflect" so that one can understand the manifestations of God's Names and Attributes, which are in operation in the universe. A sincere belief can be exhibited by submission both internally in the heart and externally by outward practice of worship and prayer.

The six articles of faith, or the pillars of belief, are the following six things in which a believer is expected to maintain belief:

1. One True God (Allah)
2. Angels

3. Books (Divine Scriptures)
4. Prophets
5. The Resurrection and Afterlife
6. Divine Decree and Destiny

ONE TRUE GOD

> "Am I not your Lord?" They said: "Yes, we bear witness."
> (Araf 7:172)

Islam addresses to the primordial nature and calls mankind to remember the affirmation given before creation, as stated in the above Qur'anic verse. Every human being is born into this world with this pure innate nature, thus he or she is naturally guided to belief in the reality of One God.

The reality of God who is the One, Eternal, and Absolute is the essential creed in Islam. God is beyond all duality and association, beyond the differences of gender and of all qualities that distinguish beings from each other in this world. Yet He is the source of all existence and all cosmic and human qualities as well as the End to Whom all things return.[33] One of the most-frequently recited verses of the Qur'an, *ayat al-kursi*, (the Verse of the Throne) lists some of God's essential names and attributes by which He makes Himself known in the creation:

> God, there is no deity but He; the All-Living, the Self-Subsisting (by Whom all subsist). Slumber does not seize Him, nor sleep. His is all that is in the heavens and all that is on the earth. Who is there that will intercede with Him save by His leave? He knows what lies before them and what lies after them (what lies in their future and in their past, what is known to them and what is hidden from them); and they do not comprehend anything of His Knowledge save what He

wills. His Seat (of dominion) embraces the heavens and the earth, and the preserving of them does not weary Him; He is the All-High, the Supreme.

Islam affirms the Unity of God and His indivisible sovereignty over the universe. God is the Creator, the Master, the Sustainer of all that exists. Everything operates according to His plan.

He has revealed, through His prophets, the Right Path for the guidance of mankind. All prophets (peace and blessings be upon them) have preached the same message:

> We never sent any Messenger before you except that We revealed to him, saying, "There is no god but I, so worship Me alone. (Anbiya 21:25)

The prophets invited men and women to a life committed to virtue, purity, justice and peace, and to act according to the guidance He has revealed.

All prophets, from Adam, Nuh (Noah) and Ibrahim (Abraham) to Musa (Moses), Isa (Jesus) and Muhammad (peace and blessings of God be on them), taught the same religion of acceptance of and submission to God and commitment to peace. Mankind's failure lies in not protecting and preserving the teachings of the earlier prophets.

As such, Prophet Muhammad, peace and blessings be upon him, was raised to restate the original message, to present it in its perfect form and to preserve it in such a way that the word of God would no longer be confused with the word of man.

> Nothing is like unto Him. (Shura 42:11)

This short verse emphasizes that God is not of the same kind as those who have been created, and therefore He is beyond all human conceptions of Him. So He has no mates, nothing is like Him, nor does He beget nor is He begotten. Nothing—neither matter, nor space, nor time—can restrict or contain Him. And this is why His Attributes—His Hearing, Seeing, Knowledge, Will, Power, Creating, and so on—are also beyond anything we can conceive.

The Prophet Muhammad was asked by his contemporaries about God; the answer came directly from God Himself in the form of a short chapter of the Qur'an, which is considered the essence of the unity or the motto of monotheism:

> Say: "He is God, the One and Only; God, the Eternal, Absolute; He begets not, nor is He begotten; And there is none like unto Him." (Ikhlas 112:1-4)

God is loving, kind, and just. With the exception of one, each of the 114 chapters of the Qur'an begins with the verse: "In the name of God, the Merciful, the Compassionate." The Prophet says, "God is more loving and kinder than a mother to her dear child." But God is also Just.

Islam rejects characterizing God in any human form or depicting Him as favoring certain individuals or nations on the basis of wealth, power or race. He created human beings as equals. They may distinguish themselves and attain His favor through virtue and piety alone.

ANGELS

Belief in the invisible realm of existence and the beings inhabiting it is another essential of Islamic faith. Since our sensory powers are limited, it is not wise to deny outright the existence of realms beyond our senses. Also, we know so little about existence that what we do know is considerably less than what we do not. Our understanding of the nature of the universe is in its infancy and we cannot claim to know what will happen in the future. Our sciences are still in their "childhood," and the future will witness dazzling scientific discoveries and developments. The Islamic concepts of creation, revelation, prophecy, events that occur in the world, worship, the spiritual life, death, resurrection, and the central position of mankind in the cosmos cannot be understood without reference to the angels.

The Majestic Maker of this huge palace of creation employs four kinds or classes of laborers: angels and other spirit beings; inanimate things and vegetable creations, which are important servants of God that work without wages; animals, which serve unconsciously in return for a small wage of food and pleasure; and humanity, which works in awareness of the Majestic Creator's purposes. Humans learn from everything, and supervise lower-ranking servants (like animals, plants, etc.) and in return they will be rewarded here and in the Hereafter.

Angels are created from "light," not the light that we know, but light in its more refined and subtle form, which we call *nur*. The Arabic word for angel is *malak*. According to its root form, *malak* means "messenger," "deputy," "envoy," "superintendent," and "powerful one." The root meaning also implies descent from a high place. Angels are granted with a partial willpower but, unlike humanity, they are not put to test. Their positions in God's sight never change. Angels are servants of God who build relations between the meta-cosmic world and the material one, convey God's commands, direct the acts and lives of beings (with God's permission), and represent their worship in their own realms.

These beings are never promoted for what they do, for each has a fixed, determined rank and receives a particular pleasure from the work itself, as well as a radiance from worship. That is, their reward is found in their service. Just as we are nourished by and derive pleasure from air and water, as well as light and food, angels are nourished by and receive pleasure from the lights of remembrance and glorification, worship and knowledge, and love of God. Since they are created of light in its more refined and subtle form, light sustains them. Even fragrant scents, which are close to light, are a sort of enjoyable nourishment for them.

From their jobs performed at the command of the One Whom they worship, their actions for His sake, their service rendered in His Name, their supervision through His view, their honor gained through connection with Him, their "refreshment" found in studying His Kingdom's material and immaterial dimensions, and their satisfaction in observing the manifestations of His Grace and Majesty, angels receive such elevated bliss that we cannot even begin to comprehend it. In addition, only they can perceive this bliss.

Angels do not sin or disobey, for they do not have an evil-commanding soul, or ego, that must be resisted. They have fixed stations, and so are neither promoted nor abased. They are also free of such negative qualities as envy, rancor, and enmity, and from all lusts and animal appetites found in human beings and jinn. They have no gender, do not eat or drink, and do not feel hunger, thirst, or tiredness. Praise, worship, recitation of God's Names, and glorification of Him are their nourishment, as are light and sweet fragrances.

Angels are assigned certain functions. Besides those deputed to represent and supervise various species on earth and present their worship to God, there are four Archangels and other angels which have special nearness to God. Gabriel (Jibril) is the chief messenger of God. Mikail is in charge of rain, the growth of plants, and the guardian of holy places. Israfil is in charge of blowing the horn to announce the Day of Resurrection. Azrail takes away people's souls at the time of death.

There are other groups of angels known as *Mala'-i A'la* (the Highest Council), *Nadiy-i A'la* (the Highest Assembly), and *Rafiq-i A'la* (the Highest Company), as well as angels appointed to Paradise and Hell. Angels who record a person's deeds are called *Kiramun Katibun* (the Noble Recorders). Munkir and Nakir will question the souls of the newly-dead. A hadith states that there are 360 angels who are responsible for each believer's life. They guard their charges, especially during infancy and old age, pray for them, and ask God to forgive them. Other angels help believers during times of war, attend assemblies that praise and glorify God, as well as study circles held for God's sake and to benefit people.

BOOKS – DIVINE SCRIPTURES

Islam enjoins belief in all books revealed by God through his prophets as an important article of faith. Muslims believe that God revealed scriptures to His messengers as a means of guidance for them. The Qur'an is the final book that God revealed to the Prophet Muhammad. God has guaranteed that the Qur'an will be protected from any corruption or distortion. Therefore no outside material has been added to it nor has any single letter been deleted out of the Qur'anic text. Since the early periods of revelation the Qur'an has been learnt by heart by many Muslims and preserved in written form.

Muslims believe that among the books that were revealed are the Torah of Moses; the Gospel of Jesus; the Psalms of David; the Tablets of Abraham; and, finally, the Qur'an.

The Qur'an is not simply a book that equals the Bible, though there are many common points between the two. One major difference is that the original books of the Bible are not available in the form and language in which they were first revealed and only translations are extant, whereas no translation of the Qur'an can be called the Qur'an; instead, a translation is simply called, "an examination of the meaning of the Qur'an."

Anyone who has done translations knows that a certain degree of interpretation creeps into the translation and that only a person who knows the original language well can curtail this interpretation to the slightest degree possible. It is absolutely mandatory that the translator have a sound knowledge of Arabic for a Qur'anic translation to be comprehensive. There are many translations of the Qur'an available today in which believers can read and understand the message of the Qur'an.

Another point about the Qur'an is that it is not a book of history, a book of science or a book of law, though it has all those components. It is first and foremost a book of divine guidance. Also, you need to know that the Qur'an does not contain detailed explanations of the situations that prompted the revelations of its verses.

Mostly the verses are guidelines and general principles. In addition, they offer glad tidings for the good, and warnings for the misguided. They contain a number of narrations that serve to give admonitions, exhortations and warnings to mankind in general. In certain cases, the Qur'an also gives specific instructions.

The Qur'an was revealed over the 23 years of the Prophet Muhammad's prophetic career, peace be upon him, in accordance with the requirements of the particular contexts that called for divine guidance in certain issues. For this reason, in order to arrive at the correct understanding of many of its verses, we need to know the circumstances in which these verses were revealed. It is also worth repeating that the Prophet did not author the Qur'an. The Qur'an, like other revealed books, is the word of God which came in a series of messages piece by piece, and not as a consecutive narrative.

PROPHETS

> We sent among every people a Messenger. (Nahl 16:36)

Similar to Judaism and Christianity, prophethood is an important concept in Islam. If the unity of God constitutes the ideological foundation of Islam, the concept of mankind's stewardship of earth provides the operational framework for understanding the Islamic view of the creation of human beings and their purpose.

Although the Qur'an mentions only 25 prophets by name, God makes it clear that He has sent many prophets to humanity. There is no tribe or nation or race to which God has not sent His Guidance. A number of "124,000 prophets" is reported in one of the sayings of the Prophet Muhammad (the stories of Zulkarnayn, Luqman, and Uzayr are also mentioned in the Qur'an, however, their prophethood is not manifestly revealed).

The greatest prophets (*ulul azm*: Masters of Determination) are Nuh (Noah), Ibrahim (Abraham), Musa (Moses), Isa (Jesus), and Muhammad, peace and blessings be upon them all.

An outstanding aspect of the Islamic belief in prophethood is that Muslims believe in and respect all the messengers of God, with no exceptions. Since all the prophets came from the same

One God, for the same purpose—to lead mankind to God— belief in them all is essential and logical.

The belief in all the prophets of God is an article of faith in Islam. Although Jews do not recognize Jesus and Muhammad, and Christians do not recognize Muhammad, Muslims accept them all as messengers of God who brought guidance to mankind. Rejecting the prophethood of a past figure would invalidate a Muslim's belief and he or she would no longer be considered to be a Muslim.

The story of Adam and Eve is found in most religious and major cultural traditions. The way the Qur'an narrates this event is crucial to the understanding of the Islamic worldview. The main outline of the Qur'anic narration is as follows: God declared His intention to send a vicegerent to the earth. He created Adam and Eve from the same substance. They were destined to play this role of vicegerency and were endowed with the "knowledge of the things" to do the job well. Then they were put to a test and asked not to approach a certain tree. They fell victim to the evil persuasions of Satan and approached the tree. But immediately after this lapse, they repented their mistake, sought God's forgiveness and were forgiven.

It is important to point out that it was after they were forgiven and redeemed that they were sent down to the earth to play their role as vicegerents of God. They were promised Divine Guidance and were assured that those who followed the Guidance would be successful. Therefore, Adam was the first man to receive this guidance and convey it to this progeny, becoming the first prophet of God.

Some important inferences follow from this. Islam does not contribute to any theory of the "fall of Adam" symbolizing the fall of mankind. Mankind was created for the purpose of acting as a deputy on earth and he came to the world to fulfill this mission. The story of Adam and Eve represents the rise of mankind to a new assignment, and not a fall.

However, the concepts of vicegerency and prophethood are not to be confused. The role and status of vicegerency is conferred upon the human being as such, and is shared by man and woman alike.

Islam subscribes to the view that human nature is similar to the highest quality alabaster, waiting to be carved. Mankind has been created in the best of forms and everyone is born in a state of purity and innocence. Furthermore, humans have been given freedom of choice. They are free to accept or deny the truth. Every person is responsible for his or her own actions, but is not deprived of this freedom, even if it is abused. To do so would be to limit this freedom. The dangers of the misuse of freedom continue to confront humans because Satan's challenge is never-ending. The trial of Adam and Eve reveals, on the one hand, the essential goodness of their nature and on the other, their susceptibility to error. It is to safeguard human beings against this that God has provided divine guidance through His prophets and messengers.

The Prophets were all human. They had the same human qualities like eating, sleeping, finding a partner in marriage, and falling ill. However, they all shared the following common features: truthfulness (*sidq*), trustworthiness (*amana*), intellect (*fatana*), communicating the message (*tabligh*), infallibility (*isma*). Prophets represented these attributes at the highest level in their time. They were supported by miracles to prove that they were not impostors. Those miracles were granted by the power and permission of God and were usually in the field in which the community they were sent to excelled and were recognized as superiors. Every prophet stated clearly that what he received was from God for the well-being of mankind. They confirmed what was revealed before and what would be revealed after them. So the message was one and the same in essence and for the same purpose.

The main content of the prophets' message was to worship the One God as He has ordained and to do good deeds in this life. Various details about God's nature and laws would be elaborated upon, depending on each individual case relating to a particular prophet. Islam emphatically rejects the concept of the "divinity" of any of the prophets. They are essentially human beings and, although they are protected from sin, they can make minor mistakes.

A full establishment of the religion is not possible only with the divine scripture; a messenger who is a medium to convey the revelation to mankind is also necessary. Conveying the message is not only achieved by expressing the divine message in words but also by becoming the best role model, one in whom believers will have a great example as to how God's message should be understood and practiced. A very simple example of this is the prescribed daily prayers in Islam, a central pillar of Islamic life and practice, which is enjoined in the Qur'an. Muslims, however, learn how to observe it from the Prophet's practice, as these prayers are not described fully in the Qur'an.

The prophets mentioned both in the Qur'an and the Bible are as follows: Adam, Idris (Enoch), Nuh (Noah), Ibrahim (Abraham), Ismail (Ishmael), Ishaq (Isaac), Yaqub (Jacob), Yusuf (Joseph), Ayyub (Job), Musa (Moses), Harun (Aaron), Dhulfikl (Ezekiel), Dawud (David), Sulayman (Solomon), Ilyas (Elijah), Al-Yasa (Elisha), Yunus (Jonah), Zakariyya (Zechariah), Yahya (John the Baptist), Isa (Jesus).

THE RESURRECTION AND THE AFTERLIFE

Belief in life after death is so crucial to the Islamic faith that any doubts about it amount to a denial of God. God's own word in the Qur'an is the foundation of this faith. Moreover, the Prophet Muhammad, peace and blessings be upon him, explained the centrality of this belief for a person who wishes to lead an Islamic life.

We know that we have no means of knowing life after death as a perceptual experience. But God has given us certain levels of consciousness that provide us with insight into realities not perceptible through the senses. The Qur'an speaks to our rational mind when it answers the disbelievers who ask, "Who will give life to the dead bones?" The answer is, of course, the One Who created them.

In the Holy Qur'an, God appeals to mankind's reasoning and addresses our power of reflection and judgment by asking us to reflect on how rain revives the dead earth. This is something that is obvious to us; if so, how can we then deny the truth of the resurrection, when Almighty God can just as easily revive the dead bones as He revives the earth?

> It is God Who sends forth the Winds, so that they raise up the clouds, and We drive them to a land that is dead, and revive the earth therewith after its death: even so [will be] the Resurrection!" (Fatir 35:9)

The Qur'an repeatedly tells us that those who believe and do righteous deeds will be greatly rewarded in the afterlife, while those who disbelieve and do bad deeds will be severely punished.

Belief in life after death gives meaning to our life, for it tells us that this life is only a test and preparation for an eternal life.

Furthermore, we know that in the afterlife we will receive justice for all the wrongs we suffer here. It may seem that the sinful and corrupt are often happier or wealthier than the righteous, but that is only for a short time. In the afterlife they will get their due.

Belief in life after death encourages a person to lead a good life on earth, since he knows the fate that awaits him if he ignores the commands and warnings of God given in the Qur'an. In fact, belief in the afterlife is the strongest incentive for a person to lead a life of virtue here. The real road to a peaceful society can be paved only if people believe in an afterlife.

DIVINE DECREE AND DESTINY

A Muslim must believe in Divine Decree or destiny (*qadar* in Arabic). The concept of destiny used in the Qur'an means a measure or the latent possibilities with which God created human beings and all things of nature. When God created each thing, He determined when it would come into existence and when it would cease to exist. He also determined its qualities and nature. And everything in the universe, the seen and the unseen, is completely subject to the overriding power of God. Nothing can happen outside His Will.

As for human beings, they are not completely masters of their fates, nor are they puppets subject to the hazards of destiny. God gave humans limited power and great freedom, including the freedom of choice. This autonomy makes each individual accountable for his or her deeds.

We cannot know our future and, to a large extent, we cannot control it. But we can make decisions within the limits of what we can control, based on our understanding of the way the world works. If someone chooses to punch his fist into a brick

wall, he cannot claim any injustice when it hurts. He knows
that the wall exists and that it is hard. That is the reality—the
"laws of nature"— with which he has to deal. Yet the ultimate
reality is that God could make the wall disappear just before one's
fist reaches it.

Just as God created nature and its laws, He made moral laws,
and we cannot claim any injustice if we are punished for dis-
obeying or ignoring those moral laws.

The concept of destiny, therefore, indicates that we must
seek harmony with God's rules of human nature and nature at
large, and consciously submit to His will. Destiny as conceived
by Islam, therefore, does not take away our freedom of choice
and action. It is our willful choice of those actions from our
inherent possibilities that are in harmony with God's will, and
it is this earns us our reward from God.

Yet, although God set certain rules in His decree as to how
things evolve, even these things can be changed through prayer.
The Prophet stressed that only sincere prayers can change the
way events unfold, and that true worship and sincere submission to God can raise the believer above the normal ways of
nature. Prayers can and do result in "personal miracles"—events
or experiences that we consider almost impossible and certain-
ly highly improbable.

From an Islamic point of view, human beings are free for
all practical purposes. A person has no excuse for making the
wrong choice and then blaming destiny, any more than a man
punching his fist into a wall can blame the laws of nature. He
knew the consequences of his actions for all practical purposes and he shouldn't expect a miracle!

We should not worry about what God has written for us, since
we can never know it. But our duty is to strive for the best in

this world and the next. Then, good results will follow, if God wills.

As for the question of whether humans are predestined to enter Paradise or Hell, we must remember that God transcends the limits of time. He is All-Knowing of the past, present, and future. Thus He knows in advance which path—good or evil— each individual will choose and what will be his or her final destination—Paradise or Hell. But such knowledge does not mean that He makes each person choose a certain path. Knowing something before it happens is not the same as making it happen. Absolute determinism is not relevant to human actions. Consider the following analogy: authors have full and exact knowledge of the book they will write, and arrange its chapters, sections, paragraphs, sentences, and words before writing it. In this sense, destiny is almost identical with Divine Knowledge, or is a title of Divine Knowledge. Thus it is also called the "Supreme Preserved Tablet" (or the "Manifest Record"). Destiny also means that God makes everything according to a certain, particular measure and in exact balance:

> God knows what every female bears and what the wombs absorb and what they grow. And everything with Him is measured. (Rad 13:8)

> The sun and the moon are made punctual according to a calculation. The stars and the trees adore, in subservience to Him. And the sky He has uplifted; and He has set the balance, that you exceed not the balance, but observe the balance strictly, nor fall short thereof. (Rahman 55:5-9)

Practice – Five Pillars

- ➤ Declaration of Faith (*shahadah*)
- ➤ Prayer – Daily Worship (*salat*)
- ➤ Fast of Ramadan (*sawm*)
- ➤ Purifying Alms (*zakat*)
- ➤ Pilgrimage (*hajj*)

"Islam is built on five pillars; these are the testimony that there is no deity worthy of worship but God and the testimony that Muhammad is His messenger, the establishment of the five daily prayers, the purifying alms, observing the fast of Ramadan, and the pilgrimage to the House of God, Ka'ba, for those who are able."[34]

DECLARATION OF FAITH

Shahadah, the Arabic word for professing Islam or confession of faith, literally means "to bear witness." The declaration of faith is the foremost pillar of embracing Islam, for the other four pillars are, in a sense, "applied confession," or "faith put in practice." *Shahadah* is the basic creed of Islam, which comprises an attestation that "there is no god but Allah, and Muhammad is His messenger." The condition of being a Muslim is simply determined by a sincere utterance of this testimony by way of which one "bears witness" to the existence of God, that there is none worthy of worship other than Him, and the prophethood of Muhammad, and thereby embraces Islam as the truth and way of life. Despite its brevity and simplicity, this profession calls for a change in the way one conceives of the cosmos and oneself. Instead of associating everything to nature, chance, and to the self, by becoming a Muslim, one submits to the Will of God, in full consciousness of one's free will and the right to choose, so that one is responsible for willingly surrendering to God.

A person is considered a Muslim once he or she utters this statement. However, "bearing witness," essentially, is not a one-time verbal confession. All people, including Muslims, are expected to keep their faith refreshed by constantly remembering their profession during the course of their lives. The Qur'an calls for Muslims who have already proclaimed their faith and are practicing to never cease striving to "believe."

> O you who believe! Believe in God and His Messenger (Muhammad) and the Book He has been sending down on His Messenger in parts and the (Divine) Books He sent down before. Whoever disbelieves in God and His angels and His Books and His Messengers and the Last Day, has indeed gone far astray. (Nisa 4:136)

Truly, faith does not consist of a simple acceptance, confession, or testimonial. Just as there are countless degrees and ranks in the manifestations of the sun, from its manifestations of light and heat in all things on the earth, up to its reflection on the moon and then back to itself, so too does faith have almost uncountable degrees and ranks, from a simple acknowledgment of reason and confirmation of the heart, up to degrees of penetration in all the parts and faculties of the body that control and the degrees that direct the entire life of a person— from the faith of a common person to that of the greatest of the Messengers. The first degree or rank of faith is simply believing in the essentials mentioned in this verse; then comes the gradual deepening of faith, and remaining steadfast in it. This is why the Qur'an usually commands or prohibits some things after the address, "O you who believe!"; a confession of belief requires obeying these commandments, which in turn causes them to become ever stronger and deeper within us.

Faith is essentially a conviction of the heart; however, for desired integration into the Muslim community, it is advised to profess the faith before witnesses. This way, a new Muslim receives the support and assistance of the community to help his faith grow and stabilize.

God's Messenger said, "Whoever bears witness that none is worthy of worship but God, and that Muhammad is His servant and Messenger, and that Jesus is the servant of God and the son of a woman who was His servant, and was His word that He cast into Mary, and a soul from Him, and that Paradise is real and that Hell is real, God will bring him into Paradise by any of its eight doors he wishes [according to his actions]."[35]

On one occasion the Prophet was sitting in a garden. He told one of his Companions, ". . . When you meet anyone outside this garden who testifies that there is no god but God, being sure of it in his heart, give him glad tidings of Paradise."[36]

On another occasion God's Messenger said, "God has prohibited from the Fire of Hell anyone who says, 'There is none worthy of worship except God,' seeking thereby the pleasure of God."[37]

PRAYER – DAILY WORSHIP

Prescribed daily prayers, *salat* in Arabic, are the central practice that shapes the daily routine and consciousness of a Muslim. Each prayer is a series of postures in which portions from the Qur'an are recited and God is given praise and the believer makes supplications. The primary purpose of daily prayers is to instill God-consciousness in the individual. God said in the Qur'an:

> Establish prayer for My remembrance. (Ta-ha 20:14)

Remembrance of God nurtures the heart. It is the true means of happiness. God said:

> Verily, it is by the remembrance of God that hearts find
> contentment. (Rad 14:28)

When the heart falls into neglect of God, Satan establishes
control over it. Sins become attractive and faith weakens.
Remembrance of God is the antidote.

> Recite and convey to them whatever of the Book is revealed
> to you, and establish the Prayer in conformity with its condi-
> tions. Surely, the Prayer restrains from all that is indecent
> and shameful, and all that is evil. Surely God's remembran-
> ce is the greatest. God knows all that you do. (Ankabut 29:45)

Muslims pray five times a day. Prayer at different times pre-
vents people from becoming overly focused on their immediate worldly needs. It is a reminder that God is the Provider, the
Sustainer and Fulfiller of all our needs. Prayer is obligatory upon
every sane Muslim who has reached the age of puberty. But, it
is better to encourage children to start earlier to prepare their
hearts for it.

One of the symbols of Islam, *adhan*, is the call to prayer. By
singing the following words, a muezzin calls Muslims to the
mosque to pray, as the prescribed time begins:

Allahu akbar	(God is the Greatest): four times
Ashhadu an la ilaha illallah	(I bear witness that there is no deity but God): twice
Ashhadu anna Muhammadan Rasulullah	(I bear witness that Muhammad is God's Messenger): twice
Hayya alas-salah	(Come on, to prayer): twice
Hayya alal-falah	(Come on, to salvation): twice
Allahu akbar	(God is the Greatest): twice
La ilaha illallah	(I bear witness that there is no deity but God): once

The first prayer (*fajr* or *subh*) comes about an hour and a half before sunrise. It is a time when the body wants to keep sleeping. To overcome inertia in order to stand and remember the Creator requires a struggle against one's self. To do so on a daily basis is a very effective training for the self in submitting to the will of God. It is made up of four cycles (*rak'at*), the first group of two being the *sunna* prayer, and the last two being the obligatory (*fard*) prayer.

The second prayer (*zuhr*) comes around the time one would stop work to eat lunch (at least for the most parts of the world) right after the sun reaches its zenith. In addition to feeding one's body, one should also feed one's soul. It is made up of ten cycles; the first group of four being the *sunna* prayer, followed by a group of four that is the *fard* prayer, and another group of two that makes up another *sunna* prayer.

The third prayer (*asr*) is half way between noon and sunset, at around a time when people are usually taking a coffee break or heading home from work. This consists of eight cycles, a group of four makes up the *sunna* prayer, followed by another group of four that makes up the *fard* prayer.

The fourth prayer (*maghrib*) is at a time when most people are having dinner. It consists of five cycles. The first group of three is the *fard* prayer and the other group of two is the *sunna* prayer.

The fifth prayer (*isha*) is at a time when one is winding down, getting ready to sleep. It consists of 10 cycles; the first group of four being the *sunna* prayer, followed by a group of four that is the *fard* prayer, then by a group of two that makes up another *sunna* prayer. An additional set of prayers, *witr*, is offered after the *isha* prayer. It is *wajib* (necessary) prayer and consists of three cycles.

The one who wants to establish these prayers must be physically clean. There are two ways to be considered clean in Islam: Bath and ablution.

Bath (*Ghusl*) – Major ablution

The whole body, including the nostrils, mouth and head, must be washed with a complete bath before commencing prayer in the following cases:

- Immediately after taking *shahada* (i.e. after one has just embraced Islam)
- After sexual intercourse
- After any seminal discharge
- At the end of a menstrual period
- At the end of confinement period for nursing women (this is a maximum of forty days)

It is also highly recommended to perform *ghusl* at least once a week, if not more, especially before attending Friday and Eid (festivity) prayers.

As an inseparable part of every act of worship and practice of faith, one must be conscious of his or her "intention" at the start of the bath that this is for the purpose of purity and worship. The Prophet, peace and blessings be upon him, would perform *ghusl* as follows:

- Make a complete minor ablution (as if for daily prayers but with one exception: the Prophet used to delay washing his feet until the end of his *ghusl* if he was using a tub).
- Rub water through one's hair three times, letting the water reach down to the roots of the hair (if your hair is plait-

ed, there is no need to undo the plait as long as the water can reach down).

- Wash both hands three times.
- Wash the private parts and the roots of the hair.
- Pour water over the entire body, beginning with the right side, then the left, washing under the armpits, inside the ears, inside the navel, inside the toes and whatever part of the body can be easily rubbed.

Wudu – Minor ablution

The first step of performing prayer is the *wudu*. This is an act of spiritual and physical cleansing, and must be performed before commencing any obligatory (*fard*) or supererogatory prayer.

Wudu is quite a simple procedure, and is performed as detailed in the table below.

1	Begin by saying: *Bismillahir-Rahmanir-Rahim* (In the name of God, the Most Beneficent, the Most Merciful)
2	Wash the hands up to the wrists three times.
3	Rinse the mouth out three times.
4	Rinse the nostrils with water three times.
5	Wash the face from the forehead to the chin, and from ear to ear, three times.
6	Starting from the right side, wash the arm up to the elbow three times, then repeat for the left arm.
7	Using wet hands, rub them over the top of the head starting at the forehead, wiping backwards.
8	Using wet fingers, wipe the inside and outside of the ears.
9	Wash the feet up to the ankles, starting with the right foot.
10	End by saying: *Ashadu an la ilaha illa'llahu wahdahu la sharika lah, wa ashadu anna Muhammadan abduhu wa rasuluh* (I testify that none has the right to be worshipped except God alone without partners, and I testify that Muhammad is His servant and messenger)

Tayammum – Ablution with clean soil

This is a form of purification that can be performed instead of *wudu* or *ghusl* when there is no water available, if the water that is available is dirty and likely to cause illness, or if performing *wudu* or *ghusl* would cause you to miss a funeral or Eid prayer (these prayers cannot be substituted or prayed later).

Tayammum is performed simply by striking one's hands lightly over clean earth, sand, stone, or a wall then passing the palm of each hand on the back of the other, blowing off any dust, then passing the hands over the face, then striking the hands again and wiping both arms up to the elbow, starting with the right arm.

Requirements of a prayer

There are 12 requirements in order for a prayer to be counted; the first six requirements are called the Conditions of Prayer, and these should be observed before praying, while the other six are called the Obligatory Acts, or the Pillars of Prayer, which should be observed while praying.

Conditions of prayer

1. Making ablution.
2. Ensuring that your body, clothing, and the area on which you are going to pray are all clean.
3. Dressing properly, so that the parts of the body that must be covered are covered (a man should cover his body from between, at least, the navel and the knees, while a woman should cover her entire body, except for her face, hands, and feet).

4. Offering the prayers at the correct times (if for any reason one is prevented from offering the prayer at the prescribed time it can be made up later).

5. Performing the prayers in the direction of the *qiblah* (Ka'ba).

6. Making an intention to perform a specific prayer.

Obligatory acts or the pillars of prayer

1. Starting by reciting the (*iftitah*) *takbir*, Allahu akbar (Allah is the Greatest).

2. Standing up (*qiyam*).

3. Reciting passages from the Qur'an (*qiraah*).

4. Bowing over and placing your hands on your knees (*ruku'*).

5. Prostrating (put your forehead on the ground while kneeling) (*sajdah*).

6. Sitting on your heels upright (*julus* or *tashahhud*).

The performance of prayer – a two-cycle example

Some minor differences excluded, men and women perform prayers in the same way. Although not obligatory, it is virtuous to observe these differences which are outlined below.

- Stand in a clean place facing the *qiblah* and make your intention to pray by specifying the name of the prayer: "I pray the sunna prayer for God." If you are praying in congregation, then also say ". . . behind this imam."

- Say the opening (*iftitah*) takbir: "Allahu akbar"

MEN: While saying "Allahu akbar," raise your hands up to your ears, with your palms open towards the *qiblah*. Then place your hands slightly below your navel, right on top of the left, and wrap your fingers around the left wrist. Fix your eyes on the place where you will put your head rest during the *sajdah*.

WOMEN: While saying "Allahu akbar" raise your hands up to your shoulders. Placing your fingers together, open your palms facing the *qiblah*. Then place your hands on your chest, right on top of the left, but not grasp the left as men do. Keep your fingers intact. Fix your eyes on the place where you will put your head rest during the *sajdah*.

1. While standing up read Subhanakah and Fatiha (the opening chapter of the Qur'an), followed by another portion from the Qur'an (a chapter or three verses at the minimum). This recitation while standing up is called *qiraah*. Please note that in the first cycle *Audhu billahi minash shaytanir rajim, Bismillahir-Rahmanir-Rahim* is recited before Fatiha.

2. After *qiraah* comes bowing. Say "Allahu akbar," let your hands loose on the sides and bow.

MEN: Make a full bow. Make sure your head and back are in a straight line. Put your hands on your knees with your fingers spread apart.

WOMEN: Slightly bow your head so that your back is slightly inclined, your head being higher than your hips. Your knees should be slightly bent. Put your hands on your knees with your fingers spread apart.

3. Say "Subhana Rabbiya'l-'Azim" (Glory be to My Lord, the Greatest) three times.

4. Then rise from bowing while saying "Sami Allahu liman hamidah" (God has heard who has praised Him) to an

upright position, your hands loose on the sides and say "Rabbana wa lakal hamd" (our Lord, praise be to You).

5. Say "Allahu akbar," and now go to prostration—*sajdah*. Place your head between your hands, making sure both your forehead and nose touch the ground. Your toes should be bent, so the soles of the toes are touching the ground.

MEN: Position your elbows so that they are not in contact with the ground or the sides of your body. Make sure your heels are together.

WOMEN: Place your elbows so that they touch the ground. Rest your stomach on your knees.

6. Say "Subhana Rabbiya'l-A'la" (Glory to My Lord, the Highest) three times when you put your forehead on the ground.

7. Saying "Allahu akbar" rise from the ground to sitting position, wait for a moment and say "Allahu akbar" again to repeat the prostration a second time.

8. Say "Allahu akbar" and rise from the ground again up for the second cycle.

9. Recite *Bismillahir-Rahmanir-Rahim* and Fatiha followed by a portion of the Qur'an and repeat bowing and prostration.

10. After the second prostration sit upright. According to the number of cycles in a specified prayer, one sits upright after the second, third, or fourth cycle.

11. Place the palms of your hands on your knees. Say the prayers "Tahiyyat," "Allahumma Salli-Barik," and "Rabbana" while in sitting position.

MEN: Position your right foot so that it is straight, with toes bent in the direction of the qiblah.

WOMEN: Turn both feet out to the right. Place your left thigh on the ground.

12. The prayer is finished by giving a greeting of peace. Turn your face to the right and say "assalamu alaykum wa rahmatullah" (peace and the mercy of God be upon you). Then turn your face to the left and say the same greeting.

FAST OF RAMADAN

The word *sawm* is the Arabic equivalent for fasting; it means "to abstain." *Sawm* in Islamic practice signifies the conscious abstinence from the cravings of the carnal soul by willingly abstaining from food, drink, and sexual intercourse from the break of dawn until sunset in order to maintain spiritual discipline and self-control.

Fasting was enjoined in Shaban (the eighth month in the Islamic calendar) of the second year after the Messenger's emigration to Medina.

Observing the fast in the month of Ramadan (the ninth month in the Islamic calendar) is one of the five pillars of Islam; it is enjoined in the Qur'an, and is therefore obligatory. In the Qur'an, issues are handled in a general way. It is the Prophet Muhammad who provided detailed explanations of the Islamic decrees mentioned in the Qur'an, for it is he who is the foremost and greatest interpreter of the Holy Book. The Qur'anic evidence for the necessity of fasting is in the following verse:

> O, you who believe! Prescribed for you is the fast, as it was prescribed for those before you, so that you may deserve

> God's protection (against the temptations of your carnal
> soul) and attain piety. (Baqara 2:183)

This verse also alludes to the fact that fasting was a practice ordained upon believers before the advent of Islam. Its origins can be traced back to the earliest recorded religions. In spite of some differences associated with the practice of fasting in various belief systems, fasting as an institution for spiritual reasons is common to all religions and well established in Judaism and Christianity. The Bible mentions that Jesus, Moses, Daniel, Elijah, and David, peace be upon them, all fasted. Moses received the Law after fasting for forty days. Similarly, Jesus fasted for forty days in the wilderness before he was called to his ministry. Prophet David fasted every other day. This fast of David is one of the most virtuous of the recommended fasts in Islam as well. Although no longer practiced by most Christians, fasting is observed in one form or another by Roman Catholics, Orthodox Christians, and in most Protestant denominations , where it is perceived as a personal spiritual experience.

The only goal of fasting in Islam is to seek God's pleasure by obeying His Command. It is far beyond restricting food intake or purifying the body of toxins. Fasting helps Muslims attain piety as a means to be in constant awareness of God, doing good, and guarding oneself against evil.

People who are temporarily sick or traveling may break their fasts, but they must make up the days they missed. Menstruating women and women bleeding after childbirth do not fast, and they must make up the days they missed. People with chronic illnesses should feed a poor person for each day they miss, and they do not have to make the missed days. Scholars agree that pregnant women and breastfeeding women who fear for their own health or the health of their children may forego fasting as long as their conditions persist. Scholars differ whether they must make up the missed days or feed a poor person.

Fasting reduces one's desires. It trains a person in self-restraint. He becomes accustomed to keeping a watch on himself. If one can forgo what is normally lawful for a limited amount of time, one should be able to forgo what is always unlawful. It shifts the focus of one's attention from bodily needs to spiritual needs. This focus is complemented in Ramadan by the exhortation to spend more time reading Qur'an and performing extra prayers. For the fast to be rewarded, refraining from food and drink must also be accompanied by refraining from unlawful acts. The Prophet said, "Whoever does not give up forged speech and evil actions, God is not in need of their leaving their food and drink."[38]

Feeling the pangs of hunger should also make a person empathize with those who feel hungry not as a matter of choice but because they can't find enough to eat. Thus Ramadan becomes a month of giving charity as well as fasting.

Fasting is obligatory on healthy, adult Muslims only in Ramadan. However, there are a number of other days when it is recommended, such as three days at the middle of each month, and every Monday and Thursday. Regular fasting helps to maintain the state of mind achieved in Ramadan.

> Ramadan is the month in which the Qur'an (began to be) revealed, providing guidance for human beings, with clear verses to guide and to distinguish right from wrong; therefore whoever witnesses that month shall fast it, and whoever is sick or on a journey, the same number of days which one did not observe fasts must be made up from other days. God desires ease and does not desire difficulty for you, that you may complete the total number of fasting days; glorify Him

in that He has guided you and that you may give thanks.
(Baqara 2:185)

PURIFYING ALMS (*ZAKAT*)

Charity is systematized in Islam in various forms. While *sadaqa* (charity) is voluntary, *zakat* is incumbent upon every Muslim who has a certain amount of wealth. *Zakat* is derived from *tazakka* which means "to purify." *Zakat*, thus, denotes keeping one's wealth cleansed and sacred by giving 2.5 per cent to the poor. This consequently makes the believer and his wealth grow in purity and sincerity (Tawba 9:103). Purifying alms is a very important pillar of Islamic practice and this is confirmed by its association with the daily prayers (*salat*) 82 times in the Qur'an.

Charity is a merit encouraged by all divinely revealed religions and other belief systems. Islam does not forbid obtaining possessions, which is the nature of mankind; but Islam enjoins the rich to share their wealth with the poor. God is the only true owner of everything and He has assigned a rightful due for the poor over the wealth of the rich; therefore, to declare a claim over one's possession and to refuse to share with the poor is in fact confiscating the rights of the poor and is a violation of human rights.

> Satan frightens you with poverty and bids you into indecencies (to spend thereon), whereas God promises you forgiveness from Himself and bounty. God is All-Embracing (with His mercy), All-Knowing. (Baqara 2:268)

God, on the other hand, has promised that wealth will never be decreased by charity.

> Say: "Surely God enlarges provision for whom He wills of His servants, and restricts it (for whom He wills). Whatever

you spend (in God's cause and in charity), He will replace it.
He is the Best to be sought as provider with the ultimate
rank of providing." (Saba 34:39)

Zakat is an obligatory form of charity taken from one's savings. It is not an income tax, but a savings tax. Its major recip-
ients are the working poor, who cannot meet all of their needs
without some additional help, and the destitute, who cannot
even meet their basic needs. It is also used to pay off the debts
of those who are unable to pay off their own debts, to free
slaves, and ransom prisoners of war.

Zakat is also an important virtue of Muslims and God warns
those who fail to observe it of "a painful punishment," as
described in the following verses of the Qur'an.

> The believers, both men and women, are guardians, confi-
> dants and helpers of one another. They enjoin and promote
> what is right and good and forbid and try to prevent the evil,
> and they establish the Prescribed Prayer in conformity with
> all its conditions, and pay the Prescribed Purifying Alms.
> They obey God and His Messenger. Those are they whom
> God will treat with mercy. Surely God is All-Glorious with
> irresistible might, All-Wise. (Tawba 9:71)

> Those who hoard up gold and silver and do not spend it in
> God's way (to exalt His cause and help the poor and needy):
> give them (O Messenger) the glad tidings of a painful pu-
> nishment. (Tawba 9:34)

PILGRIMAGE – THE HAJJ

> Pilgrimage to the House is a duty owed to God by all who
> can afford a way to it. And whoever refuses (the obligation
> of Pilgrimage) or is ungrateful to God (by not fulfilling this
> command), God is absolutely independent of all creatures.
> (Al Imran 3:97)

The fifth and the last of the five pillars of Islam, the Hajj, is observed by a journey to Mecca to join the largest human assembly on earth. The Hajj is a sacred journey from the mundane to the spiritual and it is a reminder that we are on a journey in this world. The Hajj is a believer's full submission and universal prayer, where believers shed their normal dress and put on plain clothing, until all those present resemble each other in piety and humility. It is best described in the words pilgrims chant while circumambulating the Ka'ba (the large rectangular structure):

> Here I am, O God, here I am, at your service.
> You have no partner. Yours is all praise and gratitude, and yours all dominion.
> You have no partner. (*talbiyyah*)

> ... "Our Lord, grant us in the world what is good, and in the Hereafter what is good, and protect us from the punishment of the Fire." (Baqara 2:201)

When the Ka'ba was a built a second time after Adam, by the Prophet Abraham and his son Ishmael, peace be upon them, God ordered Abraham to call humanity to glorify Him by visiting His House (*Baytullah*). This call is incumbent upon all Muslims who can afford it once in a lifetime.

> Remember when We assigned to Abraham the site of the House (Ka'ba) as a place of worship, (directing him): "Do not associate any partners with Me in any way, and keep My House pure (from any material and spiritual filth) for those who will go round it in devotion, and those who will stand in prayer before it, and those who will bow down and prostrate themselves in worship. Publicly proclaim the (duty of) Pilgrimage for all humankind, that they come to you on foot

and on lean camels, coming from every far-away point, . . ."
(Hajj 22:26-27)

The Hajj is a turning point in the spiritual development of believers. By visiting the Ka'ba, the first place of worship built under the order of God, a pilgrim meets Adam, the father of mankind; feels the joy a wayfarer feels as he returns home; witnesses that the worldly qualities like race, nobility, wealth, status, beauty, youth are nothing but vanishing and temporary titles. He will observe humanity rehearsing momentarily an episode from the Day of Resurrection, when we will have to answer to our Lord for all we have done in life. This is why the Ka'ba becomes "a fixture and maintenance" for humanity, most of whom adopt an even more virtuous life after the Hajj.

> God has made the Ka'ba, the Sacred House, a fixture and maintenance for the people. (Maidah 5:97)

Bediüzzaman Said Nursi describes the Hajj as follows:

> The Hajj is an act of worship at a most comprehensive level. It is the key that opens up many degrees of the Divine universal Lordship's manifestation to pilgrims. It reveals horizons of Divine Grandeur that they otherwise would not see. The ensuing awe and amazement, feelings of majesty in front of Divine Lordship (caused by the spheres of worship and servanthood), and levels of ever-unfolding displays to their hearts and imaginations (brought on by viewing the Hajj's rites) can be quieted only by repeating: "God is the Greatest." Only this phrase can announce such degrees of manifestations to humanity. (The Sixteenth Word, 4th Ray)

A short description of the rites

Briefly defined, the Hajj is a set of rituals performed in Mecca and certain sacred precincts around it, in the first two weeks of

Dhul Hijjah (the twelfth month of the Muslim calendar). The pilgrim enters the holy land in a state of *ihram*, i.e. with the intention to perform the visit while observing certain rules. The rites performed during the Hajj, in fact, predate the seventh century when the religion was given its final form. During the Hajj, pilgrims commemorate the reunion of the Prophet Adam and Eve and their forgiveness at the plain of Arafat and on the Mount of Mercy, while walking the same path between the hills of Safa and Marwa as Hagar, the Prophet Abraham's wife, while she desperately searched for water for her son Ishmael.

In greater detail, the Hajj includes the following rites:

- *Ihram:* Getting into the state of ihram and doing nothing that is forbidden during the time of the Hajj (sexual intercourse, disputing, wearing any clothes that have been stitched together, killing any animal, cutting any green grass or trees). Men wear a ritual garment made of two pieces of white seamless fabric.

- *Waqfa:* Staying in Arafat until sunset on Dhu'l-Hijja 9, the eve of Eid al-Adha (the Festivity of Sacrifice). Staying in Muzdalifa between dawn and sunrise on the Eid al-Adha for at least one hour. Muzdalifa is located about 20 kilometers from Mecca and 10 kilometers from Arafat.

- *Tawaf:* The seven circuits of the Ka'ba.

- *Sa'y:* a rapid walk between the hills of Safa and Marwa near the Ka'ba.

- *Jamarat:* Throwing seven pebbles at each of three stone columns (*jamarat*) in Mina where the Prophet Abraham rejected Satan.

- Sacrificing a sheep any time within three days after throwing pebbles on the first day of Eid al-Adha, and shaving or cutting some of their hair within Mecca's sacred precincts. Women only clip a little of their hair.

CONCLUSION

Islam is the divinely prescribed "how-to" manual for this world, to put it in the simplest way. It is a faith which is inherently easy to practice, and in total compliance with the natural make-up of humanity and the entire universe. In its present size, this book is intended only as an introduction to Islam. Although it covers the essentials of belief and practice, readers are warmly invited to study further by reading the Holy Qur'an, and by consulting other publications and scholars for a deeper understanding of the religion. Below is a partial list of suggested titles published by The Light, Inc. to which the reader may want to refer:

The Messenger of God: Muhammad	by M. Fethullah Gülen
The Essentials of the Islamic Faith	by M. Fethullah Gülen
Living in the Shade of Islam	by İsmail Büyükçelebi
The Words	by Bediüzzaman Said Nursi
Questions and Answers about Islam	by M. Fethullah Gülen
The Resurrection and the Afterlife	by Ali Ünal
Fasting in Islam and the Month of Ramadan	by Ali Budak
The Qur'an with Annotated Interpretation in Modern English	translated by Ali Ünal

FORBIDDEN AND LAWFUL

The Islamic life of worship (*ibadat*) and social relations (*muamalat*) govern all aspects of an individual's life. Islamic law defines all human behavior in categories like obligatory (*fard*), forbidden (*haram*), discouraged (*makruh*), and permitted (*mubah*). Here, we will cast a quick look on the forbidden things.

Contrary to general perception, Islam allows a wide space of action for believers to maintain their lives comfortably without any violation. Bediüzzaman Said Nursi puts it in a very concise way: "The limits of the permissible are broad and adequate for your desires, and so you do not need to indulge in what is forbidden." Islam accepts that everything God created is, in principle, for humanity's use and lawful (*halal*), unless forbidden by the Qur'an or the Prophet. Forbidden things in Islam can be listed briefly as follows:

- Eating the meat of certain animals, like pork, carrion, carnivorous animals, birds with talons, amphibians, reptiles, and animals slaughtered in the name of any other but God.
- Consuming intoxicants (spirits, drug, etc.) and other harmful things. A Muslim should always remain in full consciousness of his Creator and be able to address God Almighty at all times, most especially during daily prayers.

The harm which alcohol and other intoxicants cause to the individual and the society are countless and deliberate.

- Choosing clothing carefully. Islam encourages modesty, and thus extravagant dress and ostentation are forbidden. Both men and women should also be mindful not to dress in a way so as to tempt the opposite sex, such as by wearing transparent or tight-fitting clothes. In sum, the body should be discretely covered according to Islamic etiquette.

- Abstaining from all forms of gambling and usury, such as interest on loans and games of chance.

Addendum II
ISLAM AND CULTURE

Today, Islam is represented all over the world in hundreds of different countries by different ethnic and racial groups. Muslims are united under Islamic commonalities and welcome each other as members of the same family. Despite adhering to some culture-specific values, they still experience a rich diversity and remain fundamentally connected through the same system of beliefs and the same worldview. Muslims can comply with the social norms of their society, which have developed over the centuries as a consequence of regional factors, including climate, industry, heritage, national tastes, etc. The resulting variations are all acceptable provided that they have not been forbidden by Islam.

HOW TO PERFORM PRESCRIBED PRAYERS

While saying "Allahu akbar" raise your hands up to your ears, with your palms open towards the *qiblah* (the direction of the Ka'ba).

While saying "Allahu akbar" raise your hands up to your shoulders. Placing your fingers together, open your palms facing the *qiblah*.

Place your hands slightly below your navel, right on top of the left, and wrap your fingers around the left wrist. Fix your eyes on the place where you will put your head rest during the *sajdah*.

Place your hands on your chest, right on top of the left, but not grasp the left as men do. Keep your fingers intact. Fix your eyes on the place where you will put your head rest during the *sajdah*.

Make a full bow. Make sure your head and back are in a straight line. Put your hands on your knees with your fingers spread apart.

Slightly bow your head so that your back is slightly inclined, your head being higher than your hips. Your knees should be slightly bent. Put your hands on your knees with your fingers spread apart.

Then rise from bowing to an upright position, your hands loose on the sides.

Go to prostration—*sajdah*. Place your head between your hands, making sure both your forehead and nose touch the ground. Your toes should be bent, so the soles of the toes are touching the ground.

Position your elbows so that they are not in contact with the ground or the sides of your body. Make sure your heels are together.

Place your elbows so that they touch the ground. Rest your stomach on your knees.

After the second prostration sit upright. According to the number of cycles in a specified prayer, one sits upright after the second, third, or fourth cycle. Place the palms of your hands on your knees.

Position your right foot so that it is straight, with toes bent in the direction of the *qiblah*.

Turn both feet out to the right. Place your left thigh on the ground.

ABOUT THE AUTHOR

S üleyman Eriş was born in 1973 in Istanbul, Turkey. He graduated from Uludağ Faculty of Theology in 1997. He has been working as Imam for the Cosmos Foundation of Georgia since 2002.

He is currently working on religiological comparison of two Turkish Scholars, Said Nursi and Fethullah Gülen for his MA degree at the UGA. He is also the author of several articles in scientific magazines. He lives in Georgia with his wife and 3 year old child.

Notes

NOTES

[1] İsmail Büyükçelebi, *Living in the Shade of Islam*, The Light, Inc. NJ: 2005, p.5.

[2] Roger Du Pasquier, *Unveiling Islam*, The Islamic Texts Society, Cambridge: 1994, p. 7.

[3] Akbar S. Ahmed, *Islam Today*, I. B. Tauris, London: 2001, p. 24.

[4] Büyükçelebi, 2005, p. 4.

[5] Seyyed Hossein Nasr, *The Heart of Islam*, Harper San Francisco, NY: 2002, p. 9-11.

[6] *Hadith qudsi* is a saying of the Prophet that is not part of the Qur'an in which God speaks in the first person through the mouth of the Prophet.

[7] Bediüzzaman Said Nursi, *The Words*, 11th Word, The Light, Inc. NJ: 2005, p. 133-141

[8] Especially beauty and perfection that is admired by all and beneficial to others. (Tr.)

[9] Like the Bible, the Qur'an mentions that God created the universe in 6 days. However, the Qur'an never mentions mornings and evenings, and presents "day" as a relative period whose measure is unknown. See 22:47, 32:5, and 70:4: (Tr.)

[10] The original word translated as "Lord" is Rabb. It denotes God as One Who brings up, trains, educates, sustains, and administers His creatures. Note: It must not be confused with the Christian understanding of "Lord," namely, Jesus Christ as the "Son of God." (Tr.)

[11] God's vicegerency is defined as humanity being the "means" used by God to execute His commands on earth and ruling on it according to His laws.

[12] Islam considers a person to have reached the "age of discretion" when he or she becomes physically mature.

[13] Ibn Hanbal, 5:441.

[14] Muslim, *Imarah*, 37.

[15] Ibn Hajar, 1:165.

[16] Bukhari, *Iman*, 22.

[17] Muslim, *Fada'il as-Sahabah*, 63.

[18] Joseph Hell, *The Arab Civilization*, p.10.

[19] Ibn Hisham, *Sirat al Nabawiya*, 1:282.

[20] *From Towards Understanding Islam*, by al-Mawdudi (edited and summarized) I.I.F.S.O., 1970, 69-60.

[21] Tirmidhi, HN: 3069.

[22] Darimi, *Sunan*, 2:533.

[23] Ibn Kathir, 3:80-81; Ibn Hisham, 1:313.

[24] ibid. 61.

[25] Yildirim, ibid., 66-70; al-Salih, ibid., 65-73.

[26] Quoted by A. Karim, *in Islam's Contribution to Science and Civilization*.

[27] Pakistan Quarterly, vol. 4, no. 3.

[28] For these quotations, see Abul A'la al-Mawdudi, *Towards Understanding Islam* (Kuwait: IIFSO, 1970), 69-70, footnote 1.

[29] Abul-Fazl Ezzati, *An Introduction to the History of the Spread of Islam* (London: 1978), 378.

[30] Sir Thomas Arnold and Alfred Guillaume (eds.), *The Legacy of Islam* (Oxford, UK: Clarendon, 1931 [1947]), 9.

[31] *Indiculus Luminosus*, trans. by Dozy and quoted by Ezzati, *Introduction*, 98-99.

[32] Quoted by Ezzati, *Introduction*, 235-37.

[33] Seyyed Hossein Nasr, *The Heart of Islam*, Harper San Francisco, NY: 2002, p. 3.

[34] Bukhari, *Iman*, 1; Muslim, *Iman*, 20.

[35] Bukhari, *Anbiya*, 47; Muslim, *Iman*, 46; Tirmidhi, *Iman*, 17.

[36] Muslim, *Iman*, 50.

[37] Muslim, *Iman*, 45.

[38] Bukhari, *Sawm*, 8.